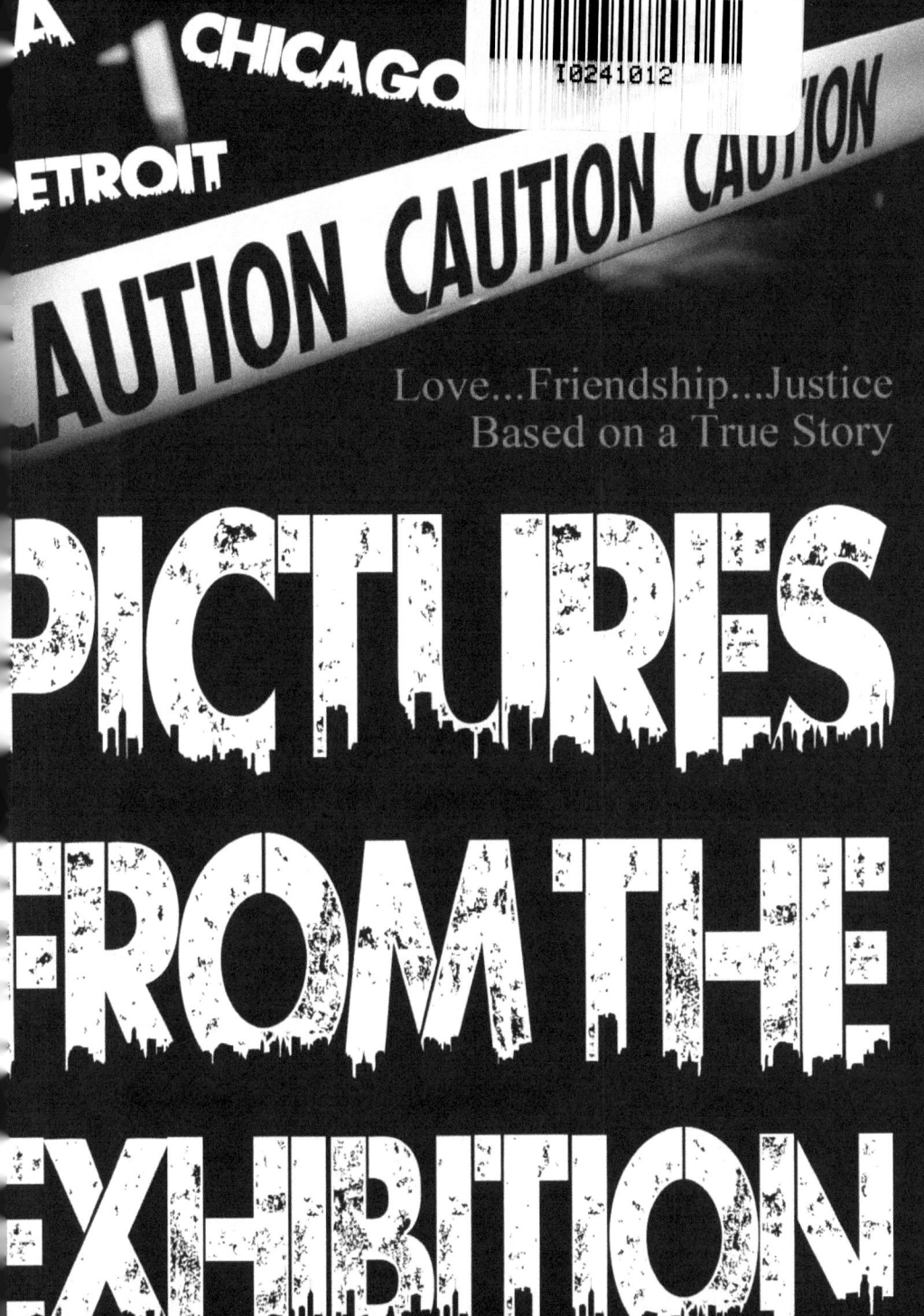

Written by: Mark Wolodkowicz

mark@jarofdreams.com

Translated by: Ksawery Swiecki

Edited by: John Hook

PICTURES FROM THE EXHIBITION

For Pawel, Patrycja and Nina

Detroit, Michigan

PICTURES FROM THE EXHIBITION
ISBN 978-0-9834700-6-9
Copyright © 2012 by Mark Wolodkowicz

Published by Mocy Publishing, LLC.
Website: www.mocypublishing.com
Email: info@mocypublishing.com
Phone: (313) 436-6944

All rights reserved. Except as permitted under the United States Copyright Act of 1976, no part of this publication may be reproduced or distributed in any form or by any means, or stored in a data base or retrieval system, without the prior written permission of the publisher.

From the author

I have not come to this world to look up to lousy politicians or vulgar priests. Ignorance and shadiness cannot stand in pair against wisdom and common sense. I believe nothing and accept what I can see or touch. I do not plan future based on the past. I live and want to be surrounded by those who live, not pre-plan.

I am in this world not to feel guilt. Everything I've done and will do is a reflection of myself and myself alone. I am not concerned about what others will say about me. Rules and regulations mean nothing to me. I live and this is my chance to be.

I am undefeatable for there is no beginning and there is no end. How can one kill what's been dead already or what is yet to be born?

Marek Wolodkowicz

Dressed in long black gown, with faces covered with black veils women were walking down the street in tiny steps. A group of men in white tops debated politically but now and then it was easy to see how politics gave room to sport. Their gestures revealed the theme to be soccer. Kids covered in mud and dust kept running around aimlessly. Store signs nearby could be understood only by few. The few included those fluent in Arabic. At first glance one could think it's Beirut or Baghdad and only the cars passing by reminded that no, we're not somewhere in the Middle East but...Well, where else in the world could one find a place where everything looks like in Arabic countries and yet it is distanced from there by thousands of miles? The city is Dearborn in the United States, the State of Michigan.

In a barber shop a man wrapped in white towel was getting a cut. He did not fit the surroundings; Caucasian, well dressed he wore a golden watch while Arabic barber was finishing his haircut with particular precision and one of the kind devotion. It had to be someone important or a close friend of the stylist. Although they spoke in English, their accents made it obvious that they were not Americans.

"Thanks so much," the barber said.

"Oh, that's nothing," the stranger replied.

"What you mean *nothing*?" barber continued, "You've found a job for my daughter. I am very grateful."

"Nah, seriously, that's no big deal," stranger answered, "an opportunity came along so I referred her for the position."

"Oh, don't be so modest," the barber went on, "I know you had been looking for a long time to find something for her. Why do you even bother doing these things? You don't get anything from it?"

"Well, I do it because I like you all and besides I feel great getting a haircut at your place."

The barber nodded with disbelief.

"So, how do you feel about the Iraq war?" the man asked. The barber stopped for a while with the haircutting and said,

"How do I feel about it? Does it even matter how I feel about it? In this shitty country here you can say what you wand and think how you like but the problem is nobody is listening. I don't know how this happens that people think one thing while the government that is supposed to represent them does exactly the opposite. Folks stay to themselves and the government to itself."

"I agree," the man replied. "The whole world has changed and it's hard to even tell who is who or what they want. American government scares the people with terrorism but they never really give the reasons why terrorism happens. And it happens because of this same very government and all of its agencies scattered all over the world. Information is false and one lie chases another. Journalists – they also gave in the pressure from the government. There really is no more true journalism, more of a repetition of the existing facts. I'll give you an example with Iraq. Some idiot from one of the agencies wrote to Washington Post bout how they are getting ready to produce nuclear bomb in Iraq. He sent the same thing to the White House. The journalists, reporters, instead of sending someone overseas to check the info, called the White House to confirm it. The White House confirmed and the next day the front pages of the newspapers were filled with photos of nuclear explosions while the headlines said something like *Iraq one step away from nuclear weapon production*. Not bad, huh? Even Iraqi government and Saddam himself had no clue they were so close to having the bomb. I tell you more; they didn't know they even had atomic program like that. That same day the White House announced that based on credible information presented by Washington Post, the U.S. government is certain that Iraq is trying to obtain atomic bomb. That's how this whole mess became credible. Nobody even moved to check any of that out. That same way reports on biological and chemical weaponry came about. Eight months after that the U.S. Army launched attack in Iraq."

The barber listened to all this with interest. After a while spoke

"I knew they were messing with something but I didn't know how they did that. What you're saying sounds incredible but I believe you."

"You believe me? But you are a Muslim and I'm Catholic." The man said smiling.

"Oh screw religion!" The barber exploded, "You're a good man and so what difference does that make if you're Catholic or a Jew? You're a good man and that's all that matters. Let me tell you a quick story," he continued.

"Go right ahead," the guy encouraged.

"There was once a very prominent scholar of Quran. He lived by his religion and observed all of the laws of the holy books. His religious demeanor gained him much respect among people. He also was much respected among the clergy who even saw him as some messenger of Allah. When once asked what was his most secret dream, this – let's call him a prophet – said: *I want to be laid to rest up there with all of the most renowned prophets, those who only come to this earth once every thousand years. This is how I would like to be recognized for my observing of the religion and for my way of living.* One night Allah himself came down and made appearance to the man saying: *You want to be one of those few buried in the land of eternal glory and prosperity? Come, I'll show you this land.* The prophet, fascinated, asked Allah: *Can I take some witnesses with me who would later on give testimony that I am indeed the chosen one?* Allah responded: *You could do that but I don't suggest you do...* Why not? – The prophet asked, *My whole life on this earth was based on the premise that one day I will be recognized some day.* Allah only said: *Of course you are recognized and yet I would not suggest you taking any witness.* The prophet took the advice and did not take witnesses with him. Allah was leading him through the clouds to that gorgeous place were only the most noble found resting place. Once they arrived the prophet saw a field filled with name tags of those very best. H came up to the first one and picked it up, the next one and the next... He looked behind and saw no end to the field of those name tags. They were covering it all the way till the horizon. There were tons of them; millions or perhaps even billions of them... *What is this?* He asked Allah. *This is the place you've dreamed of*, Allah responded. *But I thought only the best from the best were to be here; those like me, who pray and live free of sin*! Allah asked hearing this: *Who told you that the best ones are only those who pray and live free of sin?* The man answered: *What you mean who? The books! The books and the priests said so!* Allah said: *Apparently God thought something else*. The man wanted to say something but at this very moment opened his eyes. He woke up dripping sweat. He then awoke his wife.

"Did you see it?" he asked. *Did I see what?* The wife answered surprised, the *place where the prophets are buried*. She responded: *You had a dream or something*. The prophet went silent as thoughts kept running through his head. He debated "Well, maybe it is different after all... Maybe God doesn't judge us, for why would he if he created us the way we are. What sense would it make to judge someone for doing what he was meant to be doing?" And he exclaimed: *Yes, this is the answer! I have to stay who I am!*

The barber finished his story while the stranger listened, thinking deeply. After a while he cut the silence:

"This is very interesting"

"You fit that type," the barber said, "You are whom you were created."

"Hmm," the stranger began, "I have never thought of myself in those terms and I don't really want to. This is all too deep of an approach to reality, for my taste."

"Well, just think what you want," the barber replied, "I know what I'm talking about. The cut is done and you can now return to your reality."

"How much?" the man asked.

"Huh?" the barber responded with a sign of distaste. "I'm not taking any money from you."

"If you don't, I'll be upset," the man replied.

The barber looked at him and knew the man was not even close to being jocular here but quite the opposite – he looked very serious.

"Twelve dollars," the barber finally said.

"Here is fifteen and please keep the change," the stranger handed the money. Bothe men relaxed now and the smiles returned onto their faces.

"I will see you next time;" the barber said and the man responded with warm "See you, my friend."

He walked out on the street where the fresh air combined with gorgeous sunlight put him in excellent mood. He walked down the road listening to his own steps: "One, two, one, two, one, two, three, four, one, two." From whatever the source, the music appeared in his imagination. Surprised himself by it, he instantly liked the feeling. He didn't want it to stop and the calmness he felt was so strong, it made him pass by his car as opposed to stopping by him.

He just kept on walking, with no purpose, feeling the rhythm of life. It seemed to him all of his all dreams where coming true right in the beat of this rhythm and he felt the harmony linked to melody of his existence.

This is my life - he thought - the life that is a part of everything that surrounds me. All this is so fascinating; I wish I never had to stop. The air I breathe gives my existence strength, to live through the moment and I don't have to worry about anything, whatever was or whatever is yet to be. I am, after all, a part of this beautiful organism that knows exactly my place regardless of what I do or what I think. Oh, my music - play for me, play and let me live though this moment after moment, leading me to where there is no more time or space. Take me to infinity, to the eternal abbeys of being who I am; a breeze, a sunray, a drop of rain. I am nobody and I have no duty to worry about the future. I am the free and immortal ion of the universe. I love this sensation. This is true love, the happy one with no limits and no demands. I love... for me and for my own joy of loving. Yes, I love, lover all of it.

A man's voice awoke him from this daydreaming session.

"Hey you! Watch it or you'll be sorry!"

He regained focus right away and looked ahead. Two decent built cyclists did not seem to plan on making him the way. Black leather studded jackets, dark shades in glasses and bandanas on their heads spoke of their personalities. The man did not feel like having a conversation so turned slightly left to go by one of the thugs but this one was not giving up and obstructed his way once again. The man did not attempt to go by again; with quick move he punched the first one in the throat and right away got a hold of the other one's arm and twisted it out. He took him down to his knees, took a swing and broke the arm over his knee. He then came back to the first guy, helped to catch a breath and with a punch to his crotch took him down to the ground. Now the both were lying on the pavement; one unconscious while the other one moaning in pain. The stranger calm has searched their pockets, took all their money, put in his own pocket, fixed watch on his wrist and continued on in direction of his car. Silver Corvette took off slowly at first from the parking lot and loudly wheezed a moment later with its 500 horse powered voice.

Nobody on the street asked why, what reason, what price? Has violence and death become so common we no longer even feel like asking? We fear death and we fear violence yet we why do we accept it? Hey, is there anybody out who gives a thing, who cares? Anybody cares to see the difference between good and evil? Hello! Is anybody there yet?

* * *

Walking out of the airplane Andrzej saw the big sign "Welcome to The United States of America". *Yes,* he thought, the great America, *I wonder what it is like after so many years of being gone…*

Custom officer took passport from him, looked carefully at the photo and then at Andrzej himself; the photograph once more and with smile on his face returned the passport saying,

"Welcome back home, Mr. Prokop."

Andrzej didn't say anything, just smiled back at him and walked away with passport in his hand. Quickly he walked towards the restroom. His heart was pounding and the chest seemed to make out of space noise. He walked into the stall and closed the door. With his hands shaking he emptied his jacket off passports. He had three of them. He frequently changed names and not to disguise or hide from authorities but for the simple pleasure of being whom at the very moment he felt like being. Today he made a mistake and whipped out the wrong passport but luck was with him and the officer did not bother to compare the name with the one of the passengers' list. He would have been busted and only because of his own carelessness. They probably would make a terrorist out of him and put him in a can. Nobody would believe him or that he was doing that for the pure feeling of freedom. He, Andrzej, the citizen of the world would have been sentenced in a free country for terrorism of which idea he has never been able to accept.

He left the restroom and the heartbeat regained balance. He walked slowly and eventually smile returned on his face. *Life is beautiful*, he thought.

The automatic door opened loudly. Andrzej walked out of the airport and waved at the taxi cab. He opened the door and sat in white Chevrolet.

"West Bloomfield, please," he said in proper English.

"This will be around sixty dollars," the driver warned.

"Just drive, don't whine," Andrzej said squeezing a hundred dollar bill into the driver's hand.

"No problem!" he responded visibly happy.

Andrzej sat comfortably and lit up a cigar, cracked the window open. Fresh air breeze put him in sentimental mood.

"No need to rush," he told the taxi driver, took a long puff off of the cigar and closed his eyes.

America, he thought, *I should not like it here and yet something keeps me coming. There something from a woman here; the more she seems to not care, the more we care and desire.* He took a glance at the freeway: I-94 East. He closed his eyes again and resumed daydreaming.

* * *

Judge was sitting with expressionless face in his comfortable chair listening to the prosecutor as if it were weather forecast. Only on occasion he would look at me but it really meant nothing to me. It just didn't matter if he had any sympathy or hatred. Once the prosecutor was done my attorney took over. He spoke how the accident I had caused really did not cause any severe damage, that the woman who was in the other car did have her leg broke but after all I was the one who suffered the real harm and how never again I would touch alcohol as this was enough of a lesson for me.

What you are mumbling there, I thought. *What is this 'never again' nonsense? Nobody will be telling me what to do. If I want to have a drink, I will have a drink, period.*

My thoughts were intruded by the judge.

"Would you like to say anything to the court?" he asked.

"Yes," I began, "I would like to say how sorry I am for what has happened, for the accident and also express my sincere sympathy to the lady and I hope she will recover well and be able to enjoy a healthy and good life."

The courtroom went silent. Judge flipped through papers and after a brief moment looked around the courtroom and said,

"I do understand your situation but I also must recognize circumstances of this lady here. You were the one driving drunk. This was your offense and in light of the law I hereby sentence you to two years in prison without the possibility of parole."

Wham! – Sound of the gravel concluded it all. Deputy came up to me from behind and handcuffed. I instantly clenched my fist but let go after a second. Once I left the courtroom they put me also in shackles and now like a criminal I dragged myself towards the exit. Outside a small minivan awaited us; initially designed for eight people they shoved fifteen of us in it now. Smell of sweat and nicotine gave expectation of rather unpleasant commute. During the drive one of the inmates threw up.

"Swallow!" others yelled at him, "Swallow, or we stuff you with your own puke."

The guy did not care though but kept on throwing up wherever and once finished he broke down in a melt down.

"What are you crying for?" I asked.

"I need a shot," he answered, "a shot of vodka or at least a small glass of beer. Please, please," he whined.

The second guy, sitting in a corner just stared on the floor. He shakes so bad I get chills just looking at him.

"What's wrong with you?" I asked.

"I'm having withdrawals; heroine is coming out. My heart is pounding so loud I hear it in my head. I see things… It feels awfully hot too."

"It feels hot?" I repeated his statement, "but you're shaking as if you're about to freeze. Aren't you cold?"

"No, it's not cold," he said, "Muscles are demanding heroine. I'm doing here. I'm not going to make it to the can. I'll be finished."

Suddenly I felt some warmth on my back. At first in one spot but soon it started to spread around. I though maybe some idiot was smoking and the fire somehow got on my shirt. I jumped off to the aside and what I saw was beyond my wildest expectations. Dude behind me simply pissed on me. Yeah, he took a leak right on my back.

"What are you doing, dumb-ass?!" I screamed, "I'll bust your brains!"

"Don't!" he yelled back, "I just couldn't hold any longer. There is no room here. The cop isn't going to stop thinking we want to go O.W.L. I am sorry. I just had to."

I sit there curled up not knowing what to do. A voice behind me:

"First time?"

"First time what," I asked back.

"First time going behind bars?"

"What do you care?"

"I don't," stranger replied, "I just wanted to chat."

"Chat about what?

"You look smart and I wanted to get some advice," he continued.

"Advice on what?" I kept the conversation going although did not feel at all like talking to this character. A sparkle of hope in his eye and so he began to talk:

"I know the great secret of Lake Michigan," he stopped looking at me.

"What are you looking at? I said, "Go on."

"In 1796 on shores of what today is Muskegon a British ship sank with ten tons of gold on deck."

"Wow, isn't that something?" I smirked.

"Don't be sarcastic," he whispered, "I can make you my partner and we'll recover it all."

"No problem," I said, "Do you have the coordinates to the shipwreck's location?"

"What coordinates?" the strange man said surprised.

"Well, you know, coordinates; like geographical components, the width, the length," I answered.

"Oh yes," the "discoverer" replied, "You talk crap as if geography had some degrees; long and wide ones on top of it. What do you think that I'm stupid or something?"

This opened my eyes completely as I realized that he was simply retarded and for a brief moment I actually thought maybe fate has sent fortune down my way.

"What did they bust you for?" I asked the "discoverer".

"Bank robbery," he said.

"For how long had you been on the run away?"

"For about half hour."

"Half an hour?" I exclaimed. "Someone snitched on you?"

"No," he answered reluctantly.

"Well, what happened then? Talk!" I yelled.

The "discoverer" hand his head low and started to mumble:

"I walked into a bank and pretended to fill out the deposit slip. I whipped out a fake check and my ID, filled out the slip and just observed. Suddenly it got quiet and empty around. I thought 'now'. I pulled out a gun and ran up to a chick at the desk. I put the gun to her head and screamed: *Pack the cash into the bags and throw on the ground now! If you don't, I'll shoot him!* They listened; threw the cash on the floor. I picked it all up and ran. I jumped into my car and home I drive with no slowing down. Happy I get to my house and there they were already, waiting.

"Who was waiting?" I asked.

"The cops, of course. Who else?"

"How did they get there?" I keep asking.

The "discoverer" just nods his head left and right.

"Well, how did they get there?" I ask again.

"Well go on, dummy. You started, you might as well finish!" voices resounded around the van.

The "discoverer" evidently stressed out said:
"I left my driver's license on the table at the bank. The moment I left they called the cops and my address."

I was stunned. I didn't know if I should laugh or cry?

What am I doing here? – I thought - *An alcoholic, a drug addict and an idiot, and I'm in the middle. How great is that. What have I done to deserve this?*

The cell is 10 by 6.5 feet; concrete floor with bars both up front and in the rear, no windows, a toilet bowl, a shelf for clothes and little table. Tiny. Some bug crawls up the wall. A guy in the next cell hums some melody. Quite the voice he has. I am on the fifth floor and through my bars I can see the cell across the giant place. We are divided by an empty, five stories

Large space filled with murmur of prisoners. They are on every floor. Five hundred of them in the building. You can hear the Latinos, the Blacks communicating in their own code and what about me? I am lying on the prison bed and conduct my own deliberation. I'll be here for another two years, locked twenty three hours out of a day just myself on my own. They will let me out for meals for five minutes and once a day for an hour long walk outside. What to do with the time? It is 10 p.m. and the guard is yelling out his time out announcement. The lights go down and the inmates, as if in a tease attempt, begin to talk louder and louder, some yell to each other, some sing even louder. In other word: chaos. I don't think anyone is asleep and I don't get this situation. Why aren't they trying to get some rest but go wild instead? I'm trying to sleep but it isn't easy. The noise is seriously disturbing and I am getting anxious.

They act like a herd of fools, I think to myself.

My inner voice starts to makes sense to me after a while, in its own, slow pace.

You are in prison, among criminals, alcoholics and druggies. Some of them are here for murders. DO not expect human instincts or anything that used to be considered a norm in where you come from. How did you get here if you don't feel that you belong to this company? Nobody was inviting you. You kept on demanding it. Now live with your decisions.

My inner voice causes fatigue but I still feel relaxed. I have nothing to worry about tomorrow, absolutely nothing. I, therefore, will not worry about anything. Yes, no worries about anything from now on.

I closed my eyes. Life pictures begin to dance in front of me peacefully, as if in slow motion.

Yes, I'm thinking, *my dream about freedom is coming.*

* * *

Clerk at the counter had a dirty apron on but his warm smile was making up for it.

"How can I help you," he asked.

"I want a keg of beer," I said.

"Sure, no problem but you will have to pay for the keg deposit."

"That's fine," I answered.

"Come on guys! I got it!" I am yelling to my friends. The came up quickly and we put the barrel down on the ground. We started to roll it to the camping site. The fun was unbelievable. We drank and talked about all kinds of things. Somebody played some guitar. The guys more and more frequently were leaving for a moment behind trees to ease their bladders. The girls did but not so frequently. Somebody was trying to tell a joke but no one listened. Me – I enjoy the sound of the guitar and it soothes me.

"Ok, let's go," I heard.

"Wait a minute," I mumbled back.

"Oh, come on. I am tired and you can barely keep your eyes open."

"What are you talking about?" I got irritated, "You mean those few beers I have had?"

"Nice way to put it – *few*. Why not to just say few gallons?"

"Oh, come one, don't be like that. It's been great here, hasn't it?" I kept defending.

"Great? Just look around you. Everyone is drunk. They barely can stand on their feet. Those two over there got in a fight and this one keeps chasing that poor girl as if he wanted to just rape her. The guitar player puked his guts out and you are close to just falling asleep right here on the grass."

"Stop pissing me off. You're always like this when I have a good time."

"You call it a good time?"

"Ok, fine. Go to the tent and I'll be right over."

She left. I got up and I did feel I had drank but not to the point of not knowing how to enjoy the good time. Instead of going back to the tent I took off and went to a party in town. It was great in the club; the girl laughing dance and so seductively I decided to join in.

"Give me your hand," I said to one of them.

She did and now I turned her around by her waist and grabbed once the twist was over. My turn now. I twisted around in a spot and brought her closer to me. Our lips met in passionate kiss.

Far away, I heard the distant sea murmur. The girl was looking at me and kept on thrusting, harder and harder unable to reach orgasm. Covered in sweat I passed out right next to her on the sand.

"And…Did you come?" the strange girl asked.

"I did," I lied to her. I wanted to just get up and run away somewhere where nobody could find me.

"Come on," I said, "I'll take you to your tent."

We kept on walking when in the distance I saw shapes of two men. They resembled some of my friends but I was wrong. Those were the locals hunting for the tourists.

"Hey, buddy," they started, "We're going to borrow that doll of yours and have a little fun with her."

I knew where that was heading; I'll get beat up over some girl I don't even know, whom I had met an hour earlier and yet already managed to sleep with. Oh well, it is what it is; maybe it won't hurt too badly.

"Just try, you punks, and you'll be looking for …"

I didn't get a chance to finish when the punches began to pour down.

"Happy birthday!" My friends are chanting as I am turning eighteen today. Everyone envies me for the ability to go and legally buy booze, vodka, wine, beer and nobody can say anything. We exchange hugs; wishes of prosperity and health keep on pouring. She is standing to the side and I really, really like her but how to stir up a conversation?

"Hi," I say to her as I APPROACH.

"Hello," she greets me back, "Nice party you threw there."

"Thanks so much. Would you like something to drink?"

"I'm not sure I should."

Great, I'm thinking, *I may be able to get her drunk.* "Of course, you should,:" I say, "Let me get you something."

I went to the kitchen and added some zero proof to the wine. It worked mighty fast and I don't even remember how soon we ended up in the hallway. I pulled down her pantyhose and rushed myself into her fast and passionately. It was done and over quickly. She went to the elevator and left while I returned to my company forgetting about her. But...I liked her so much, didn't I?

The next day was the rerun of the drinking spree. Buddies brought the wine over and it was time to "get over the 18th B-Day hangover", right? Emptying one bottle of wine after another we mentioned a friend who drunk went to the zoo to feed the bison and got killed by one of them. Later on

We also talked about somebody else who bet he could drink a gallon without stopping once. He did and died an hour later.

There was no end to reminiscing while the alcohol kept stirring up our emotions.

* * *

I was awoken violently by the alarm sound loud so bad I thought I would go deaf.

"Get up! It's five o'clock!" The guard was screaming, "Breakfast at six!"

Entire wing of the prison was lit up and it took a while before I could regain my senses where I was.

I took off the tan top and washed my face over the sink, rinsed the teeth along the way.

The bars in front of me opened up loudly and I felt great release being able to get out of this hole. We are taking the stairs down from the fifth level down. Everyone looks tired but that's no surprise – they didn't sleep. What about me? I think I slept. I had dreams.

There are 160 or so feet to the cafeteria and that's the time to chat or have a smoke. Everyone is lighting up heavily. We talk about our achievements before getting here. Coming to the cafeteria the guard informs,

"You have two minutes to finish your meal. No leftovers are to be taken back to the cell." I do what I can to manage eating what's mine. I did. After lunch I get out for a walk. I have a whole hour. I take a spot in line to the telephone booth. There are five hundreds of us, inmates, and only thirteen phones. After three days I have reached my destination. I call my fiancée.

"Hi," I say once she picked up.

She didn't ask about anything, just complained how hard things are, how she has no money, that the car broke down, about the pain in her groin and how she will have to see a doctor. I put the phone down without a word. I returned to my cell and the bars shut behind me just as loudly as when they opened. I laid down on the bench and closed my eyes. Pictures from the past began to arrive slowly.

I laid down on the bench and closed my eyes. Pictures from the past began to arrive slowly.

The dream about freedom is coming, I thought.

***

The ten story tall, concrete building, the inseparable symbol of socialism, shines in the sunlight. The life-giving star can turn a beast into beauty. In front of it a number of cars parked; there are Ladas, Fiats, Syrenka as well as the ever popular "pawns" fiats. The elevator slowly makes it to the sixth floor. There are voices resounding in hallways, coming from one of the flats. I cross the threshold; right to the front of me is the bathroom and the large room to the right. I come up closer; a group of people is sitting at the table and eating something. I see the telephone in the corner. Swarzedz-made furniture was testimony to somewhat well—to-do family living here. People were very welcoming and friendly. They probably know me and like. I just stand – not sit, and listen to the conversations: farming problems, building of the new school, difficulties with the production increase… Those were some of the "men's" subjects. Women cover fashion, kids, etc. Typical social affair is taking place.

"Listen, honey," a woman said to a guy.

"Yes, dear?" he - probably husband - replied.

"The vodka is almost gone. Would you go to the store? She asked.

"Right on, let me just put something on," he excused himself.

While leaving, he made a general inquiry:

"There will be none of the "Czysta" left at the Mart, so what should I do?"

"Just get whatever they will have, as long as there's something we're good,
 one of the men said.

The rest of the guests seconded him loudly chanting and rushing the man so he gets back fast. Once the booze is gone there isn't much to talk about.

It is midnight and everyone is engaged in heated debate. Over and over someone screams "have another one!" Women begin gossiping about men. One of them gets up on the table and starts to dance pretending to be a go-go girl. Guys are more openly covering political themes.

"We'll get rid of them communists and start everything anew!" the yell, "We're strong and educated, and the youth will support us. It is going to be a paradise here!"

One of the guys put his head down to the palms of his hands and napped. The other one shares "dirty" jokes. It's chaos. Somebody came up with the great idea to put some music on. The sounds flow in and some begin their dancing attempts. They stumble and dancing just isn't working. They come back to the table and have another round.

"Cheers!" they scream.

"Cheers!"

"Anybody wants some food?" a woman asked.

"Nah," the voices declined.

"Give us another half over here," a guy in the corner asked.

"Wow, can you drink or what?" the woman commented.

"Ha ha, it takes a fifth for me to begin feeling better."

You're not kidding. One couldn't even tell you drank anything."

The man smiled widely with clear expression of pride. He poured another shot and drank.

"Whew!" he whispered, "Nasty. Come on, give another one over here." The women looked at each other and busted out laughing.

A woman one gently tilted the door open and walked into the room.

"Are you sleeping?" She asked.

"No," I answered.

"They will leave in a moment."

"I hope so," I said.

"You're not mad, are you?"

"No, mom, I'm not. Tomorrow will be my time to go party."

"Just don't drink too much, ok?" The woman asked.

"I won't. I promise," I responded.

Two days after this particular gathering, the host, my father, died of a heart attack. He was found in his office at work. The cops quickly conducted and concluded the investigation. The doctor told me that dad had had many problems at work, that the "Solidarity" was acting out again and that those were some tense times for all of us to the point that only booze allowed for a short break from reality. For the first time in my life I thought that maybe vodka helped my father part from this world forever.

A seventy years old woman sat at the table surrounded by people in their 40's and 50's.

"What would you like to drink, auntie?" A question came.

"You have some booze don't you?" She answered with a question.

"Sure, we do!"

They filled up a glass and the woman drank it all at once.

Well, come on, get me another one," she asked.

Everybody looked around at each other. They poured her another one and she drank it. Not a half hour passed when the elder lady begin to lose control of her movements. After an hour, she blabbed about subjects put of the blue. One by one, however, she just kept on asking:

"well, get me another one here.
She wanted to get up but stumbled and lost balance. One of the guys grabbed her. They took her to the taxi cab and she took off home.

"How is she going to get to the door?"

"How ill she find her key?"

"How will she get the clothes off of herself?"

"How is she going to make the bed?

I opened my eyes. I was covered in sweat.

My father. My mother, I thought.

What a nightmare that was. Good thing it is over now. The lights went on and the guard yells:

"Five o'clock! Get up! Breakfast at six!"

I got up faster than yesterday, washed up my face and now have some time to shave. Brushing my teeth I looked ahead. I see the bars open on the opposite side of the building. The inmates leave for breakfast. They walk calm, one by one, towards the steel staircase. Suddenly something happened. I saw it but it seemed so incredible I just stood in my cell stunned. The hollow thump of the human body falling on the concrete brought me back to reality. I came up to the bars. He was lying in blood. Yes, I witnessed him falling down. Why did he fall down? I don't know. Did he jump? Did someone push him? Did he trip over something? In my sub consciousness, for a split second I have impression there were two of them. Who was the other one? Perhaps it's better not to know.

The guards closed all the cells – no breakfast today. They have to clean up. I look down from my fifth floor; they clean off the blood and drag the body along the hallway. I feel sad and I feel like throwing up. I sat on my bunk.

He didn't even yell or scream, I'm thinking, *didn't move hands. Maybe he wanted to die. Who was the one next to him? Maybe those were some dirty paybacks. Maybe there is a maniac looking for the next? I am scared of death, afraid of dying. Did he have time to say farewell to this world? Did my father know he was dying? Does mom know the risks of drinking?* I closed my eyes. Slowly the colorful images began to arrive.

Yes, I'm thinking, *my dream about freedom is coming.*

***

Priest spoke slowly and with much attention to the words. He talked how I was about to promise love, respect and that I would not leave in the hour of need. At the end he asked if I wanted her to be my wife.

"Of course, I do," I replied.

I am twenty one years old and married. She is three months pregnant. I am still not through with school and yet we are already married couple. Deep inside I am happy that I'm about to be a father but isn't it too soon? She threatened to take her own life. I felt bad and plus – it's about keeping the word. You didn't think when you were doing so now do as you think, ha ha! We put the bands on our fingers; kiss and it is all done and over with. Some fifty or so years ahead of me... We walk gracefully down the alley to the exit and I stare at the people around face by face. Here's auntie and there's uncle, cousin... Suddenly my eyes paused on the face I did not know, a girl's face. She had dark, maroon hair cut to the shoulders, green eyes and lips pulsating with lust for love and betrayal. I look at her and just can't stop. My imagination is at work. I can see her in my arms and how she tells me with the kiss to take her. I want her for myself only, so she can become a part of me.

"What are you thinking about?" My wife asked.

I awoke.

"Doesn't matter." I replied.

The wedding was very loud. Only 30 people made it though. The darn martial law would not allow for people to leave their towns and villages. Nevertheless everything turned out very nice; great food and booze, chats about politics. At midnight the cops paid us a visit to see if we conspire against the communism. The told us to wrap everything up within half hour but nobody took it seriously. All of my guy friends are still bachelors and it is just I – always first, unsatisfied, with the sense of pride and great ambitions. I have a wife and baby on the way but I cannot find myself in all this. Yet I have always wanted to travel, to play the guitar and make love to girls. What is awaiting me? Job, furnishing of the place, a car, kids.

"Well come on, get some over here!" I yelled to a friend. He eagerly ran up with the bottle.

"Ah, there you go, Mr. Man, drink now; it's going to be different from now on for you.
"What are you talking about? We'll still be able to get together like in the old days."

"Nah, that's what they say but the reality is different."
I drank a shot of "Czysta" but I didn't like it. I poured another one. That one didn't do me either. There went the third and the fourth…

It was June, nice and warm. She tilted the window and screamed"
"Look, it is so beautiful!"

Yes, it is my daughter and I am proud of her. At last she is mine and will always be mine. The nursing staff did not allow me for a prolonged window viewing and left. I ended up going home. When I got there a surprise waited for me; all of my friends gathered together to wish me all the best and congratulate on the daughter with wishes she makes me happy.

Vodka was pouring everywhere. My mother – a grandma starting today – did not waste any either. My friends kissed their girlfriends making promises to be fathers soon as well. Girls on the other hand talked about various wedding fashions. After few hours everyone just passed out. Vodka defeated us all. The company ended up sleeping through in my flat; some straight on the floor and others on the bed. I myself laid down on the couch in the small room; next to me a buddy of mine and on the other side two girls. Suddenly I felt somebody messing around my zipper. I grabbed the wondering hand and held on to it.

"Let go. I want you now," she whispered.

I let go. She skillfully pulled my pants down and sat on me. I was concerned that others may wake up but nope – they were out of it asleep like stones. Once it was all over I myself zoomed out. At dawn she was already gone.

The second child came to the world after a year; son - the heir and successor. The plans, the dreams I have had for him – I cannot count. His birth was celebrated for three days. Everyone pointed out the resemblance to dad. I was thrilled.

The situation in Poland was, however, miserable. I saw no future for myself, not to mention the kids. Friends were leaving West one after another. I still believe there will be changes in Poland and things will get better. I want to believe but the facts point otherwise. Poor kids – what is awaiting them?

A terrible scream has pulled me out of deep sleep in an instant.

"Five o'clock! Get up! Breakfast will be in a moment. It is Sunday and those of you who want to attend Service must sign up in the cafeteria!", the guard was yelling out.

So it goes, right from the beginning over again, I thought.

I did, however, sign up for church Mass. After lunch the bars opened up and I left the cell.

The church was on the other side of the prison and so I was able to familiarize myself better with "the neighborhood". The prison itself consisted of several tall buildings, five storeys each and numerous one storey barracks. Altogether: six thousands inmates. It was like a small town where everyone, although stranger to each other, was connected and bound by the unwritten rules of the prisoner. I walked into the church and the guards checked me thoroughly. I sat down in the third row. It was not a Catholic per se church but Christian. We read the Bible and the pastor interprets the holy words. Suddenly my neighbor on the row pokes me on the side.

"What do you want?" I asked.

"I have something for you; let go of the jacket a little," he responded.

I don't know him and I'm not sure what to do. He doesn't really give me a chance to think and puts something solid underneath the jacket.

"Somebody will pick it up from you by the bloc."

I want to say something but he puts his fingers on the lips and whispered, "Hush.. Hush…"

I have no idea what's underneath my jacket now. I am getting scared. I get the feel of the object and gather it is a foot long peak of a blade. *If they catch me here with this I have guaranteed extra two years in here*, I think. I no longer listen to the pastor. I want to leave but I do have to make it to the end here. My heart is about to flip out inside me. I am walking. The guard makes a step towards me. Panicking I'm thinking how I will explain my possession. He passes by and checks the guy behind me. My walk regains some confidence. A group of inmate behind me yells "Good job, Euroguy! Good job!" A linen cart obstructed my way. Some Puerto Rican rushed up towards me and in split second put his hand underneath my jacket and grabbed the blade. I did not protest one bit and all he said was "How are you, amigo?"

After all those events the dinner tasted like nothing else in the world. I was in excellent mood hence I gave my apple to the neighbor from the next cell. He was very happy.

We make our way back to the bloc and from afar the distant I see a group of guards surrounding something lying on the ground. I walk up. On the ground lying was an inmate. He looked dead. Suddenly something bothered me. I looked again at the body and in the back sticking out was the same blade that just a few hours before was in my possession.

"Don't stop!" A guard yelled out.

I kept walking towards my block while the thoughts were racing in my head. I laid down on my bunk assessing the day. I close my eyes. Slowly, in full gallery of colors, the pictures began to come.

Dreams about freedom are coming, I thought.

***

I'm landing in Italy. It is a beautiful day with some 70 degrees while Warsaw was freezing in way below sub grades. I pass my customs inspection and proceed towards exit. I spot my friends and we begin to lose ourselves in each other's arms. Later on was the long road to the camp. I look around; everything new, nice... I register in the camp office. When asked where I wanted to go, "To the U.S.A."I replied.

The whole procedure took about twenty minutes and I left the building holding in my hand brand new ID. I wasn't thinking about my wife, not my children. I walked into a room with ten beds in it. Everyone welcomed me asking about Poland and so I put down on the table a bottle of vodka and begin my storytelling.

They listen carefully and are pleased when I tell them that things are getting worse and worse in the old country. It helps to survive here, in this misery on site. The camp is awful, dirty and what not. Time after time one could hear arguments and drunken mumbling. Every now and then there is a fight or a blow up of some kind. Some cannot make it through and return. From the cafeteria, where cats travel on tables snooping through the bowls with food, I come back to my room. They asked if I wanted to play some cards. I took upon their offer and we began to play drinking at the same time. Once the vodka bottle emptied we switch to wine. A tall and well-build fellow came into the room. Everyone knew him and he was quite tanked by now. He walked around the room whining while we kept on playing. Suddenly for no apparent reason the stud grabbed a knife and now has it by the neck of my game partner. The situation got a little complicated and everyone is quiet except for the buff who says,

"Tell me that you love me. Tell me that I am a good man. Well, come on, tell me that."

The guy with the knife on his neck is in no mood for a conversation. He sobered up instantly. On his neck drops of blood began to appear.

"Well, of course, he loves you," I said, "We all love you. Aren't you one of us, after all? Now, stop this knife ordeal here and sit down, and have a drink with us."

A consternation; silence was cut by the stud,

"What do you guys have to drink?"

"A little wine," I responded.

"Here you are," I said and pushed a glass in his direction.

He put down the knife and sat at the table. Everyone's mood started to come back and the guy continued to talk.

"Wow, that was dumb. I wanted to just scare you but later on I just couldn't stop playing this crazy part."

"Oh, so you were just bluffing?" the guy with now wounded throat screamed out. "You're an idiot! That's all!"

I walk down the hallway drunk, passing by some guy from Slovakia. I know him and he is a cool fellow. I don't really pay attention to him now and just keep going to the camp store. I pay the money and get a quart of wine. I dislike myself. The wine no longer tastes good. Why do I keep buying then?

We drank until the dawn. The card game doesn't do the time killing trick and we wander through other barracks to find some ladies' company. We bug the Czechs, the Hungarians but nothing worked as they could tell we were drunk. The next day we found out that the same guy repeated his knife incident with some Bosnian guy. It didn't go well though and he got bit up so badly that he ended up in a hospital for two weeks able to recognize his face in the mirror after a month.

I am so hangover I am scared of everything. I enter the office of a woman who directs the immigrants to the U.S. I'm trying to be nice but the booze took away all my charm. Hangover makes impossible any attempt of communication. I answer her questions but cannot way till the moment I can leave and have a drink of beer or wine.

I spent my money on beer and had six of them. By now I no longer can buy a ticket for my train back to the camp. I go on the train anyway, without the ticket but I get caught and thrown out at the nearest station. I have about 15.5 miles to walk to the camp. While walking, I sobered up I made a promise to myself that I would never again touch this, vodka, wine, beer... Never. The first thing I did when I walked into my room was grabbing a bottle of wine and drinking half of it at once. *Much better now*, I thought.

I walk to work – dealing with grape bushes. They pay five dollars per day. I go because I need money. One has to eat and, sure thing, drink.

I dig around those damn bushes and think about when the day will be over. OI have awful blisters on my hands and I can barely hold on to the barrow. Final, at last and I finally can board the bus. They let me out in front of the camp and went to do some shopping. I had baked chicken that I ate in the park so that nobody could see – sometimes people like to "join". I had two beers and I want to sleep but how can you when the barrack is just shaking from all the drunken parties going on?

Like everyday a guard yells that it's now five o'clock and we better hurry up because the breakfast is at six. I get up and rinse off. Meanwhile the guard came up to my cell bars.

"Hey, Euroguy, this is your last day in the 'tower'. They move you to the barracks."

I was stunned. *Finally*, I thought.

They only lock us up for the night in the barracks. During the day the cells are kept open and one can use the shower whenever. The gym is also available.

This is luxury; I'm thinking to myself, *I will start working out*.

Every hour you have to report back at the cell as they keep count but that doesn't bother me at all. I am glad. There are also three telephones in the barracks available whenever. I call my fiancé but the phone is silent. I call again in an hour but it's no different. I try the next day. The operator said the other party answered but once they found out the call was from the penitentiary they hang up. I no longer make the call. I just keep coming to the gym; starting with small weight but raising the bar. I like it. It gives me strength and not just physical but also the spiritual. Today, for the first time, I benched 242 pounds. I'm happy.

I laid down on the bench and closed my eyes. Pictures from the past began to arrive slowly.

Yes, I thought, *my dream about freedom is coming.*

* * *

The plane got caught in turbulences. It's shaking really bad. We circle the Kennedy's airport in New York waiting for permission to land. I'm scared the whole thing will just fall apart and we'll end up all dead. I'm scared of death. My friend next to me is sound asleep. He is totally tanked. We make the landing and through the window I can see the Concorde. I have twenty four dollars on me and America is all wide ahead of me, ready to be contested. It's June 26th and I will remember this day for a long time.

I mop floors in a super market, scrub toilet bowls and make my first dollars. I got promoted. Now it is tearing down a huge brewery and free beer. I drink every day. I got promoted. Now it's paint jobs and installing gutters on houses but… I am no longer happy with myself. I know I can do better. What is holding me back? I go to the bar to have a drink. There are hundreds if not thousands just like me, here. There is this conviction in America that as long as you keep working nothing will happen to you. I hate this physical job. I can't do this, don't know how and I feel no satisfaction. The next payday and I send the money to Poland; to the wife and the kids. I got promoted. I now work in my field, fixing radios and TV sets.

I try to bring over the wife and the kids. First I have to make sure they have roof over their heads but that is not an easy thing – I make pennies.

All my pass time I spend in the Polish club and everything comes down to just drinking beer and vodka. In our conversations we cover trivial themes and pretend to be experts in the fields. I feel that I am not the person I should be. What is holding me back from pursuing my dreams? Do I have dreams? What is the way to make some money? Who should I become? What job to take up in order to feel some kind of satisfaction?

The questions are multi. I order another beer to chase. Tomorrow will be another hangover but I do nothing to avoid this.

I wake up next to a girl I don't remember. How did I meet her? We sleep with each other from time to time. She says I'm her "type". SO what? I don't care about her.

I opened up my first business and I have an employee. He is English. I am happy that a Brit is working for a Pole. After work I go to see the girl and we drink vodka together. Later on we make love and in the morning I return with another hangover I go on to continue building my future. I'm unhappy with myself. I don't like my lover. The business isn't going well. I drink every day. On the outside people perceive me differently, though.

"Look," they say, "Such a hard working guy; he will be well off one day. It's just a matter of time."

The first business failed. I started another one. It failed. The third – failed. People start giving me advices to stop these trials and just go to work for somebody else but I can't. Something keeps telling me *Listen to yourself*.

The wife and the kids make it over here and I'm very happy. I teach the children to swim and bike. I respect my wife and don't cheat. My daughter's birthday – vodka is pouring down. My son's birthday – we celebrate in similar fashion. My birthday – we drink for two days straight. My buddies never fail – they never turn down the booze. Children's Communion celebration – we drink. We go to the beach – we drink. How can I afford all this booze?

My new business is doing better than expected. I can afford the new house. I have two cars and the kids go to better schools. This needs to be celebrated. Everyone at the bar is ecstatic to see me and I buy everybody around. The barmaid is very pretty. I leave large tips. We end up in bed in a month. Damn it, I have fallen for her. I love this barmaid and I care that she is with me. She is different than others; doesn't drink and listens to what I have to say. I myself stopped drinking as well. A year has gone by without a drink and I am feeling much better. I am still in love with the barmaid and I think she is the one, the one I have been waiting for.

The divorce case didn't take too long. After the years of marriage I am all alone again. The barmaid insists that we get married but something is stopping me. A good friend of mine shot himself. He had too much one day, drank more than he should and just called it quits. The second buddy burnt in a car when he drove home from work one day. The third had a heart attack and died in his garage, finishing the third bottle. I continue to stay sober but I am not happy. I have the money. For the first time in my life I am in the position when I can afford pretty much anything. Full of myself I once went to a bar to have a just a glass of cognac. It burnt in my throat and in my stomach. I left the establishment and went home. Three days later I had a small glass of cognac again. A day later there was a glass of wine. On the next a bottle of beer found its way. Some other time tea with a bit of rum to taste. I didn't even notice when I have fallen for this again. I was back to the daily drinking. This time though I am wealthier so I no longer go to some cheap joints. I pick expensive restaurants and high-end clubs. A glass of cognac can be twelve and a beer seven bucks. *What the hell*, I think to myself, *I can afford it now.*

The hangover is the same thing all the time. It doesn't matter I am hangover on a thousand dollars or a five dollars' worth of booze. I hate myself. I am late for the business meetings or simply cancel them. I can't stand looking people in the eyes and it feels like I'm dying. I lock myself in the house and watch TV for hours. I do not pick up the phone.

Leave me alone, everybody, I think to myself, *what did I do that it is now when I need to be left alone you all want to talk?*

I am in need of this peace more and more often. Vodka is always with me. It doesn't call me, doesn't preach to me, and just sits there patiently waiting for me on the table.

I will quit tomorrow, I say to myself every morning. The first thing that I do, however, is reach for a beer. I breathe heavily at night and sweat profusely while the heart pounds as if it were a rattle. I have to get drunk to be able to fall asleep. The great America; my wife is no longer and

I dislike my friends; I feel no shame or inhibitions; I have no scruples, no debts. What do I have?

Money and booze, I'm thinking.

"Five o'clock! The guard yells, get up; breakfast at six; if you're late you don't eat!"

I got up covered in sweat. The last dream really did me. I look through the bars and see faces of other inmates across; empty, with no smile, no hope. I have been here for six months already without touching a drop of alcohol. I do not feel even the temptation. I feel great and despite that I'm incarcerated – I feel free.

I signed up for AA meeting. Everyone here has one and the same problem. They share their lives. I feel sympathy for them but I don't feel the connection. I don't think they can help me. They're not strong enough to help me. I need somebody truly strong and disciplined, who has a sense of order and organization. It has to be someone I can trust; somebody I can confess my life to. Yes, it really would have to be someone unusual, someone who would love me, be with me always, at all times.

I know someone like this, I'm thinking, I have known her for a long time but it has never occurred to me to ask her for help.

This time I will break and ask for it. I know it won't be turned down. I just have to present my case right, with strong evidence so it speaks for itself to this person. Yes, I'm going to do this today, in a moment, now...

What are you waiting for? I asked myself, you are this person.

I laid down on the bunk, closed my eyes; slowly in full colors, the pictures began to arrive.

NO! I screamed out.

I opened my eyes, sat on the bunk and began timidly to collect the arguments I needed.

***

Let's start with how I got here. Two years in prison – this sentence should be a shocking one to me and yet it wasn't. I feel as if all this had to happen. I have always believed that the world was a product of chaos. I have thrown away long time stories about God as a man sitting somewhere up in heaven with his long, grey beard watching us. Maybe the time has come to again, think once again how did I end up in this earthly dwelling? The longer I think about things the more I'm willing to accept that perhaps it wasn't chaos that made DNA, water and chemical elements. There had to be some force with unlimited powers to make this all work.

I started to show interest in terms that I had barely used in the past: infinity, Universe, immortality, willpower and power of intent, stellar space. If the universe is pre-programmed by some energy then my existence cannot be accidental. I am, therefore, on this earth to serve some purpose. I play some role here. There has to be something that connects me with this overwhelming force. What is that link? Let's assume that the source of our thoughts and actions is constantly in some proximity to us. It is some energy that formed us and created our bodies. Yet the body is only the tool to complete our contemporary tasks in the universe. Why is it that my life is filled with unlimited amount of obstacles and why most of the time I am simply unsatisfied? I don't want to believe that such a sophisticated force made a mistake and created a human being that dwells in self dissatisfaction. I simply feel that I have somehow lost touch with the positive energy that is there to help me to be happy.

Yes, I thought, I definitely lost that touch. *I have been driven by my ego.*

I am what I own. My achievements speak of who I am. My reputation defines me. My body separates me from others. My life goes on in a rhythm but far away from things I would like to do and have. I separated myself from my own persona, lost touch with my own positive energy. Yes, this is what happened – I have lost touch.

I left the barrack. I'm feeling excited. My thoughts started to take on some for, some regularity. I am happy that I can be honest with myself. I go to the gym. Once I entered I saw an inmate there lying on the floor in a puddle of blood. I called up for a guard. It turned out that the guy with his head busted had bragged around about how he was doing time in some prison near Chicago and befriended one of the most acclaimed bank robbers. Well, others decided to test his credibility. The secret communication mechanism went on to work and the news went to all the prisons in Michigan. After some time it reached Illinois. Prisoners who worked with inmates' files there checked out the Michigan smart Alec's credibility.

"Nope," the answer came, "He's never done time in Chicago."

The communication exchange set off again and two months later everyone in our facility knew the guy was lying. When he went to work out at the gym two creepy muscle types had been awaiting him already. One, without saying a word, fired up a punch straight in his face. It took him down and the next punches followed. There would not be anything particularly unusual about it if it were not for the fact that the punches were thrown with twenty pounds dumbbells.

I worked out for about half an hour then returned to the cell. I sat down and tried again to focus.

Where was I? I'm thinking to myself for a moment. Oh, I continuously complain about being broke. I complain about my wife. My gut is distorting my posture and I don't look the way I should. I get easily excited but then get quickly tired and have no energy left. I don't like places I go to. In the mirror I see how I'm aging. I dislike my job and feel underappreciated. I have chronic cold and it tires me that whatever the new virus I am the first to become its victim. I have to be pleasant in my business, cater to everyone and please the clients; very tiresome. Whatever I do, there is always the tax office to come after my money. I like money, the feeling of being popular and to maintain the position, prestige. I also like pleasures, women, alcohol and tobacco.

Every day I repeat to myself things I don't like.

A year flew by quickly. Half of the sentence is now behind me. I work out five times a week and run twice a week as well. I play the guitar, compose and in the evenings write my poetry. I try to be kind to guards and other inmates. I teach the young ones history and geography. I've lost some weigh and feel lots of energy. I start to like myself. I don't think about my fiancé who has annoyed me by now. I don't think about my job that I have disliked. I start to understand that it is not so much what we do. What matters is how we feel. I am healthy, strong and sober. I have quit smoking also. I am sure that now, once I've started to like myself, I will be able to love others just the way they are. It is only a matter of time when the money will find me and not the other way around – me chasing it. I know I will treat my wife or my partner in a different way; instead of looking for faults I will focus only on their attributes.

I have tons of energy. I've finally reunited with the energy of the Universe which created me to begin with. I will enjoy the places I attend because I will change them according to my taste. My intuition will tell me what kind of work to devote myself to in order to feel

Appreciated and to do what will be in accordance with my destiny. I have to ignore the colds and simply ask my energy to strengthen my immune system. I will teach my child respect for all forms of life.

I am one of the kind creatures brought to the Earth for some reason.

I will, therefore, love and respect instead of hate and destroy. Everything I have done and will do is planned. Instead of protesting the energy, I will now accept it.

I have to enjoy life because I came to this world with nothing and I will leave the same way.

I walked slowly without looking behind. It is supposed to bring bad luck. There is a small bag in my hand with a sandwich in it and a check in my pocket for sixty dollars. That is all I have saved up after two years in prison.

I feel good. The bars behind my back slammed loudly. This time I know it's the last time. Other inmates yell something to me but I don't pay attention.

I need help from nobody. I know what to do with my life.

I let those dreams about freedom go. Now I am truly free. It is I, I and once more – I.

I looked up to the sky, the beautiful blue, and the infinity behind that blue. It won't let me get hurt. I will always be here and I have no need to worry about the future. There is no beginning and no end to infinity.

***

A man in his nineties walked out of the store and looked around. In slow motion he proceeded towards the parking lot. He looked very well for his age; slender, with firm walk he reached his car, searched his pocket for the key. Few feet away he spotted a group of people packing their car with groceries. Subconsciously he smiled to them not expecting anything in return. He just happened to be that way; always smiling. He felt happy for the life kept on going in its pace and despite his advanced age he was doing very well.

He was able to tend to his own needs and proud of it. He got his keys out and opened the door. He didn't even notice that a young man, maybe in his twenties, came up from behind him tall and well built. The senior saw him when the man was already right by him; wanted to ask if the young guy needed some help but didn't manage to. The young man without a word fired a punch with his fist in the old man's face, grabbed his car keys and opened the door. The old man despite the shock felt after the powerful punch did not lose his balance. He grabbed the young guy's hand and asked "For what?" The perpetrator freed his arm and fired up another punch, then another one, and one more… The punches were falling all over like rain. The guy was throwing them without looking. The old man fell down. "Help," he quietly got out of himself. The group of people saw what was going on just a few feet away from them but nobody dared to step in and help. Quite the opposite: they quickly got into their car and drove off with squeak of the tires leaving the old man at mercy of his attacker.

The man lost consciousness. The young one kicked off his tormented body, got into the car and put the key in ignition. When he grabbed the steering wheel he saw another hand on the very wheel. He wanted to turn his head over and look at the person sitting next to him but he didn't make it. He only remembered one detail and that was the gold Rolex watch on the stranger's hand. He felt a punch so powerful his entire body shook. He wanted to react but felt completely powerless.

The young guy opened his eyes. He wasn't sure whether he slept or lost consciousness. He didn't know how long he had been in this stage. He looked around to see he was in some abandoned garage.

What am I doing here? He thought. He saw the white Chevrolet. Now he remembered: *This is the car of that old man, whom I had beaten up on the parking lot. What is that all supposed to mean? How did I get here?* Thoughts were running quickly through his mind as he was trying to make some sense out of them. The process was interrupted by some voice.

"You finally got yourself together?"

The young man looked up trying to see the face of the stranger but couldn't as the man stood behind the bright light pointed in his eyes. He wasn't able to see the stranger's face,

"What do you want?" He asked.

"What do I want?" The guy seemed surprised, "I think you are the one to say what did you want before you decided to torment that old man on the parking lot."

"I just wanted to take his car for a ride."

"Well, this decision will cost you a hand and a leg," the man responded.

"What kind of nonsense is that? What leg and what hand?"

"You are an adult and you can tell right from wrong. You know what you can and what you should not do. You also know that we alone are the bearers of the consequences for our decisions and that our wrongs cannot be transferred onto anybody else but ourselves.. Would you agree with that?"

The young man listened carefully, not knowing quite what it was about but understood what the guy meant.

"Yes, I do agree," he answered humbly.

"I'm glad, I really am. You knew it was not a nice thing to do to beat up the old man but you did it anyway. He was healthy and strong, walked on his own, did his own shopping and drove his own car. He had to be in his nineties. You took it all away from him. After what you did he was taken to the hospital, got a stroke and now cannot talk, cannot go to the bathroom or walk anywhere for that matter. Everything he was proud of, you took it all away. You sentenced him to death that he was not ready to ask for.

"I didn't mean any of that," the young guy said.
"Shut up," the guy cut him off, "This is not a courtroom and nobody here wants to hear you."

"And what about you?!" The young man yelled out.

"Me?"

The place went silent.

"I am here for you."

"For me?!" The young guy screamed again, "Then let me go!"

"No," the man said in calm voice, "You're here to answer for your decisions."

"Yes, yes!" The young guy kept shouting, "And my decision now is to leave, now!"

"Go then," the strange man said.

The young guy wrestled in one place like a caged animal but nothing came out of his efforts; tight ropes held him firmly in one spot.

"Do you want to leave?" The stranger asked.

"Of course I do!" The young fellow shouted angrily.

"OK then," the stranger continued, "It is all up to your decisions."

"What decisions, you idiot?" Yelling continued.

"Well, look at yourself. You keep being an arrogant and think you just can do anything, don't you?"

"Stop torturing me. If we end up in court I'm going to say you had tortured me."

"Court?" The strange man was surprised, "So you do believe in courts and the law?"

"Yes!" The young guy screamed out.

"So what sentence would you give yourself fort beating up that old man?"

"It would be deferred."

"Ok, we will postpone your execution and give you a chance to live."

"What are you talking about?"

"Shut up now, you little punk!" The strange man now ordered, "Listen to me and will be crucial that you do. It's a life and death situation for you here, so listen. I'm only going to say it once and give you ten minutes to make up your mind. Your legs and hands are tied to the ground with chains attached to concrete logs in the floor. It is impossible to free yourself on your own so I will help you. I will let your left hand and left leg so you can move but you still will not be able to free yourself. But I will also help you with that and give you a sharp ax. This is where my assistance will end, though. Once you get the ax you will have ten minutes to cut off your right leg and hand. Then you can crawl up to the phone that I will bring and call for help. You will then crawl out from the garage and wait outside for the ambulance. If not, you will burn in here for this gasoline tank here will explode after ten minutes. It was nice meeting you, you nut-job. Now go ahead and take responsibility."

Complete silence surrounded the place. Tears came up in the young man's eyes. He was unable to say anything, just stared ahead at the bright light blinding him. Far away he recognized something familiar, right away he knew the gold Rolex. The light got shut off. He suddenly felt first his hand being free and then his leg. He shadow boxed the empty space ahead and kicked equally empty space. After a short moment he felt the cold steel on his hips, grabbed and squeezed tight. The light went back on again. The young man looked around but there was nobody in sight. He looked at

Chains which were confining his limbs and understood there was no point to even attempt cutting those off with this little ax. Further away, by the old man's car, there was a gasoline tank and a container of propane.

I must be dreaming this; he thought, *it's impossible for this to be real. It's just a dream, a nightmare that's all.*

He grabbed the ax firmly and looked at his leg, his hand after. He let it go down and looked at the nearby cell phone. *This isn't real*, thought was pondering through his head still. Suddenly he saw a flame next to the gas canister.

"O my God!" The young man screamed.

"Ahhhhh!!" he whaled lifting the hand with the ax and swinging it down.

"Ahhhhh!!" He screamed again.

The stranger opened the door of the car, sat down and started the engine. He turned the radio on and tuned to his favorite dial; techno music. He started off slowly, going towards Main Street and looked at his watch. He then stared at the mirror; a large fire glaze. While driving he wondered if what happened that evening could be called justice, the lesser of the evil or a crime?

Hmm, he thought, *Seems to me what happened is just a story of those two men; a young and an old one, whose paths crossed in those unexpected circumstance. And it could have been so differently.*

***

Andrzej woke up at dawn. He realized he had fallen asleep in an armchair, watching TV. He got up, turned the TV off and turned on the radio. He heard some rap song and quickly switched the stations. Slowly he proceeded to the bathroom. Once showered and shaved he walked up to the telephone stand and dialed a number.

"Hello?" He heard on the other end.

"Hi John, do you know who this is?" Andrzej asked.

"Am I supposed to? What the fuck am I, a mind reader?"

Andrzej smirked.

"It's me, your best friend," he said.

"You keep on talking like this," the voice on the telephone continued, "I will find your ass and beat the shit out of you. I don't have friends."

"OK, Andrzej started, "I just wanted to hear this. I though maybe something has changed in your life. People change, you know."

"People change in their graves," John replied.

Andrzej smirked once more.

"It's me, Anrdzej."
A bit of consternation took over for a moment.

"Little Andrzje? The Polish one?" The voice on the telephone asked.

"Yes, this one."

"Welcome home," John said.

"Hey, thanks."

"Are you ready to make some dough?"

"That's what I'm calling for."

"I've got something for you. The usual; 2-5 for me and the rest is for you."

"Deal," Andrzej replied and asked: "What discipline?"

"Sell-buy properties," John said.

"Sounds alright. When can I start?"

"Yesterday," John said and laughed explosively, "Come up to the club at 9 p.m. and I will give you the coordinates."

"Ok then," Andrzej said.

"Hey, I'm glad you're back, very much so."

This conversation put Andrzej in very good mood. He walked down to the garage, got in the car and started off burning the asphalt. He liked driving, enjoyed the breeze and warmth of the sun rays – all this put him in meditative state. He thought about the past and planned the future of which he no longer was scared. He was certain he had found his place. He wasn't afraid he would lose the money he yet was to have or that he would be lonely, for there are so many women in this world. He wasn't afraid of getting sick or crippled or what not. He wasn't afraid of anything. He believed he was placed in this world for some reason. He didn't know what it was yet but he didn't really care to know it either. Every day brings something new and all it takes is to notice it.

He pressed the gas pedal harder and the speedometer reached 100 miles per hour. *Faster, faster, you crazy maniac*, Andrzej thought enjoying the moments of silence and surrounded by what he loved the most, the words.

The girl was sitting behind the steel desk looking through some papers. She had long black hair and amazing black eyes. Her soft hands were flipping through the pages. Her tanned legs crossed one on top of the other created the exciting line ending on her somewhat wide hips. The phone rang and she gracefully answered:

"How can I help you?" She asked.

A woman's voice spoke on the other end. The girl listened and after a brief moment said: "

"Yes, this contract is still valid. You can model for Masrati but we still have to meet and see you." The voice on the other end continued but after a short moment the girls cut off:

"There is nothing to talk about in terms of money," she said, "Let's meet in an hour on the corner of Main and 4th St. There is a small café where I will be waiting for you."

She put down the phone and pulled her hair back. *And there I have a model*, she thought.

Andrzej exited the freeway and drove down the Main where right at the corner of the 4th St. He spotted a café. *Oh well, might as well pop in for a small coffee*, he thought. He vigorously turned left and pulled in to the parking lot. After leaving the car with firm step he walked towards the coffee shop

The girl left the studio and looked up to the sky.

Beautiful day, she thought. She gently opened her Volvo's door and sat down. While starting the car she also instantly turned the radio on and the hip-hop filled the space. Feeling the beat the girl moved in its rhythm. Soft arms moved left to right, back and forth and she tilted the window. The wind instantly breezed off her hair. She remained in this harmony feeling joy in the heart, happy to be able to live through every moment of this gorgeous day. Approaching Main and 4th she slowed down, turned right and ultimately parked next to a silver Corvette. She proceeded towards the café.

It was packed inside. People debated with each other, some busy typing on their laptops. Waitresses moved around like ants on their hill. Sounds of the espresso machine and the smell of coffee were filling the air. Andrzej kept staring at one place. *I'm lucky*, he thought. He walked up towards a table and sat down. Young waitress in her tight, black pants showed up almost right away.

"What can I get you?" She asked.

"Just a black java," Andrzej responded.

"No pastry?" She tempted.

"No, thanks. You've got beautiful eyes," Andrzej said. The waitress blushed and just said "Thank you", walking away.

He picked up the newspaper off the table and looked at the front page. The red headlines hit him like a thunder: "War in Iraq," he read slowly, "Three U.S. Soldiers Killed." He turned the page: "A Maniac Killed 30 Students On University Campus," "Priest Accused of Child Molestation," and the next page: "Mother Killed Her One Year Old." His hands became sweaty and movements inpatient. He flipped another page; the headlines screamed: "Korea Has Nuclear Weapons," looked anxiously at the next one saying: "Paris Hilton Goes to Jail for D.U.I.", and the next page: "Famine in Africa – Thousands of Children Die of Hunger." He opened the "For Sale" section. "Young, good looking girl looking to marry a wealthy man who will take care of her." Andrzej looked at the next page: "Attractive married woman looking for three-way adventures." He started to get angry.

What is this? He thought. Garbage, dirt, death. No good news anymore, huh? Nobody writes about love, good things happening, plans for the future. Thousands of years of civilization and we instead of feeling lucky to be alive continue doing everything to destroy ourselves. Is there such thing as love anymore anywhere? Men and women putting themselves out in "For Sale" sections. What nonsense. Maybe I should put an ad: "I will buy love, a true and happy one."

He took his eyes off of the paper and looked towards the door. His face focused on a girl standing by the counter; tall, black haired with long legs, hips slightly too wide hips, but what the hell, he scanned her with his eyes. All of the sudden he got up not quite sure why and started coming up to her.

"Hello," he initialed a conversation, "Excuse me. I am sorry to bother you but there seems to be no room at the café and I sit by myself – if you feel like it you can join me.

The girls listened surprised.

"I am expecting someone," she said, "but I can take upon your invitation. Meanwhile perhaps some table will become available.
"My name is Andrzej," he introduced himself and reached out his hand.

"I'm Jordan," the girl answered exchanging the handshake.

Once he felt her palm on his, he felt nice. Her handshake was gentle but not weak.

"I am very pleased to meet you," he said.

"Likewise," Jordan whispered.

They walked towards the table. Once they sat down it got quiet. Neither him nor her said anything and just kept staring at each other. This sweet silence was interrupted by the waitress.

"What can I get you?"

"I will just have a cup of tea," the girl said.

Once the waitress walked away, she spoke with a smile: "Thanks for the invitation."

He returned the warm smile saying: "It is nice that it happened. It's not an every day thing that we meet somebody whom we like very much. You are very beautiful and it had to be a good omen sending you down here today."

"What are you talking about?" Jordan was surprised.

"I just say the way I feel. Are you offended?"

"No but we have just met."

"Beauty is the beauty and doesn't need time to be noticed. You are beautiful."

"And you're crazy."

"Could be but I have no regrets."

"Let's not talk about me," Jordan asked, "Let's talk about something else."

"Fine. Let's talk about love."

"You really are nuts."

"No, I'm not. I'm just for real."

"Fine, let's talk about love. You start."

"Love," Andrzej began, "is might, but only when it comes from the heart, from our soul. Love transforms into force once we reject the heart and throw in rational thinking. Two people in love make the perfect two. They do not have problems – they solve themselves by themselves. They do not see obstacles. Why? Because they feel no need to see them. They don't need to see obstacles for the only thing that counts is love. The rest is merely a background for their feeling. They want to love, to create one, to be not just for themselves but for the entire world surrounding. They are happy to see flowers, trees; they star gaze and ream to sunsets. They love to sing and dance. This is love. When they become husband and wife their kisses cool off. Lips kiss but the heart dies out. They say "love" but that is just it: a word, without power, without passion. This is when love stops being might and becomes force dictating the types of behavior. This I can't do and that is inappropriate, and watch for the kids, and so they don't think that love is fun. Love is gone but we think it's still alive. No, it died out. The boy begins to wander with his eyes after other girls and the girl reaches out with her thoughts to that colleague from work. This is the end of love and what's next?"

Jordan listened carefully with eyes shining with some strange fascination. At some point she stopped him:

"You're right," she said, "I feel the same way although I would like to think of my love as of something somewhat different. I want to love for the pure joy of loving, seeing my man the way he is with all the good and the bad, the noble one and the liar who at night can drive me ecstatic time after time demanding nothing else from me but being the way I am. My man must be himself, live his life free from frontiers of rules and promises. He must be free and I want to love him for that holding his hand for hours without saying one word, absolutely nothing, for the touch alone should speak for the fact that we are one body and one soul. I want to desire him for being the one free eagle who at any given time can fly away or plummet. And if he flies away to the unknown, I will love him even more.

Andrzej grabbed her by her hand. She didn't protest, quite the opposite; she put hers on his palm. They were silent. After a moment they realized they had been staring in each other's eyes. Their eyelids didn't move. They looked at each other enchanted. It felt good.

The sweetness of the moment was interrupted by the waitress.

"Can I get you anything else?"

They both shook off as if kidnapped from the deep trance.

"No, we're all good," Andrzej replied, "Just the bill, please."

They sat without saying anything, waiting for something but not knowing what it was.

The waitress brought the bill and Andrzej slipped the money into the waitress hand.

"We're all set,
he said.

He suddenly stood up and said: "Thanks for everything, Jordan, I must go now. It was very nice to meet you."

Jordan didn't say anything. Andrzej shook her hand and walked off towards the door. He opened the door and looked back at the girl. She didn't look at him though, just stared ahead.
Andrzej left the café and with fast pace proceeded towards the car. He started off the engine and took off with squeaking tires. Wind was brushing his hair and massaged his face. He felt something on his cheek and reached with the hand. At first he thought it was raining but soon realized it wasn't a raindrop but a tear.

Damn it, he thought, *I've waited for her the whole life and now that she was so close within a reach I ran away. I don't even know where she lives, what' her phone number is... What an idiot!*

"Why!" He screamed out to himself, "Will I see her again?"

The traffic silenced his voice and his thoughts and fears have gone to infinity. Perhaps somewhere out there the stars will tell if something was born or just come to an end.

Andrzej drove well; fast but confidently. Slowly he regained his composure.

Whatever will be, will be, he said to himself. *If she is to be mine, she will.*

* * *

A middle aged man was sitting in his arm chair looking at the pool. It was a hot day and the wicker seat was the perfect spot for a moment of relaxation. The man reached out to the nearby table and grabbed the bottle of whiskey; poured into glass. The cherished liquor resounded pleasantly while dissolving the ice cubes.

What a beautiful day, he thought; *I wonder what the guy wants and what he is coming here for. He mentioned some sale and buy type of deal but I'm not sure… Whatever, if he bores me or tries to scam I'll get rid of him, simple. What a gorgeous day – I don't feel like spoiling it.*

He finished his thinking when he heard the front door open. In a while he saw a tall man approaching the little storm gate. The stranger opened the door with confidence, walked up to the pool and energetically to the armchair.

"Mr. Smith?" He asked.

"Yes," the man in the armchair responded.

"My name is Mark and we have an appointment.

"Yes, I know. Sit down, please."

Mark sat down.

"Please, treat yourself to some whiskey."

"No, thank you but I don't drink."

"Let's move on to the subject then. I would like to tell you though, that if you are here to try to get some money out of me or what not – forget it. My investments are successful and I really don't have the time for risky business whatsoever."

"Oh, nothing like that," Mark smiled, "I am not here to ask you for anything. I just wanted to remind you and strengthened out some details from your life."

"Straighten some details?" Smith asked with a touch of embarrassment.

"Yes, strengthen out," Mark repeated with a smile.

"I don't recall anything that would require *straightening out*."

"Allow me," Mark asked, "a certain story…"

"Go right ahead," Smith answered.

"It was 1986, L.A., two young people," Mark began.

Smith got anxious in his chair. He raised the glass of whiskey and drank at once; put the empty glass on the table and impatiently poured another one.

Mark continued.

"Two, let's call them *friends* decided to rob a bank. They had been planning it for a year. Finally they got to the point where the plan seemed impossible to fail. All the details were worked out to perfection. The moment came when they were ready. It happened; they broke in, got what they needed out of there – three and half million dollars."

Smith kept nervously drinking his whiskey; he wasn't looking at the man and his thoughts were far away, in L.A. Mark continued.

"The friends packed the treasure to their car, brand new Jeep with phony tags. They had 30 minutes to be far enough for the Jeep to be left abandoned and for them to switch to another car. Twist of fate wanted that two miles away from the bank there was an earthquake. The freeway broke in half and the two friends found each other in the middle of it with the three and half millions on them but with no way out. They picked up the bags and started off walking down the freeway. They got to the nearest parking lot and stole the first car in sight. Then they took off according to the original plan. Everything would have been great if it were not for one small detail. The camera on the parking lot caught the man who broke into the car. After many months of searches the cops found the man who broke into it. The investigation was launched and the cops concluded that this theft was related to the bank robbery. The ball got rolling and soon the man who robbed the bank was on trial. To save his own skin and got some decent plea bargain the guy snitched and told on his friend. Not only that; he also gave coordinates to the place where the money was hidden. We could say *snitch* got a year and half while his friend, whom he had blamed the whole thing on, got 15years.

"Enough!" Smith yelled, "Who are you and how do you know this?"

Mark smiled and reached for a glass. He poured some club soda and drank.

"Does it matter?" He asked, "I can see you got interested in the story, though."

"Don't play a fool! What do you want?"

"I told you what I wanted," Mark responded. "I want to straighten out some details from your life."

"Don't piss me off! How much do you want?"

"Oh no, no, no. You start being a little arrogant and that's not nice. I didn't come here for money."

Smith grabbed the phone.

"Put it down," Mark's voice changed. "Put it down or I'll bash your brain with this bullet and that will be the end of it."

Smith put away his phone.

"Now listen to me very carefully and answer my questions," Mark ordered. "Were you the one to rob the bank with your friend?"

"Yes," Smith answered.

"Were you the one to squeal on your friend to the cops for a better deal and reduced sentence?"

"Yes."

"The money you stole – did the two of you plan to open a school for disadvantaged kids in South America with it?"

A moment of silence occurred.

"Yes," Smith said.

"And did you want to teach English and business in that school?"

"Yes! Yes! Yes!" Smith kept exclaiming now.

"Can you tell right from wrong?"

Silence.

"Can you tell right from wrong?" Mark repeated the question.

"Yes," Smith whispered.

"Tell me, what was worse – to rob the bank with intent to help others or to give a friend away to the cops?"

"Giving away the friend, "Smith answered.

"See," Mark said, "now your life begins to have meaning. What do you do now?"

"I buy and sell houses," Smith answered humbly.

"Buy and sell houses," Mark repeated ironically. "What kind of houses you buy and what kind of houses you sell?" He asked angrily.

"Houses…" Smith stuttered.

"Let me help you," Mark said. "You buy houses from people who are no longer able to keep paying them off to their banks. They have lost their jobs and have no way of making the payments to banks any longer. These people go through life drama because the house, the one they had dreamed of, for which they had worked so hard is no longer their safety zone or their pillar. This home full of love and warmth becomes collateral for vultures like you. What do you do with a house like that?"

"I sell it off," Smith said.

"I sell if off," Mark repeated with disgust in his voice. "You give it back to the wealthy vultures so they, again, can offer it to some next dreamer, who dreams about the pillar, the safety zone. Look at yourself. What happened to you? You wanted to help the people, were eager to do great things. You robbed a bank to help the youth. Look at yourself – now you rip those youths off. What is the greater evil – to rob a bank or someone already broke?"

Silence.

"What is the greater evil?" Mark emphasized the question again.

"To rob the broke one," Smith said.

"See, that wasn't so difficult. Don't you think that friendship and helping the poor are the core of our existence?"

"Nnaah…._ Smith stuttered.

"Don't B.S. me here through the teeth but be a man and answer," Mark was not giving up the argument.

Yes," Smith said.

"Yes what?" Mark kept drilling. "Speak in full sentences, you moron, as I may lose my temper here otherwise."

"Friendship and helping the poor is the core of our existence," Smith mumbled.

"Ok, now listen. You were a human being once. You had a friend and helped the poor. Now you have no friends and rip off the poor. Is this good or bad?"

Smith was silent.

"Is this good or bad?" Mark repeated.

"It is good to help the poor and to have friends," Smith said with more confidant tone.

"I'm glad you came to this by yourself," Mark said. "Now tell me who you are?"

"I am a con and a thief," Smith said with conviction.

"There you go. Look at this brave self-criticism. I like it. Maybe you are a likeable guy even, after all not the boil as I thought initially."

"Where is he now?" Smith asked.

"Are you asking about your friend?"

"Yes."

"He is dying in a hospital with liver disease. Once he left the prison he never picked himself up, really. He drank; both booze and antifreeze. He drank because he wanted to die. He no longer had dreams and no longer a friend."

"Where is he?" Smith asked.

"I am not going to tell you. That would be too easy. Besides, I am not even sure if he is still alive. After the last antifreeze doze he got so sick the docs weren't giving him a chance."

"Did he send you here?"

"No. He never spoke badly about you. He was not mad or wanted to get even. I am here completely out of my own will."

"So why did you come here?"

"Well, you fuck, to try and make a creature out of you, the one you once were."

Silence and a light breeze loosened up the atmosphere a bit. A gentle sound of waves reaching end of the pool added to it.

"What do you want?" Smith kept asking.

"Four months ago somebody robbed a bank in Chicago," Mark started. "There were two people but they didn't manage to get to the main safe. They weren't that good. They took some itsy-bitsy from the drawers and such. While running away one of the guys hit the garbage can and cut his hand. There were blood spots left. The cops are looking for the guy who will match the blood type and whose DNA will match the one found on the skin tear-off from the garbage can."

"What do I have to do with this?" Smith said confused.

"Let me finish. I've watched you closely for some time now. I watched you go and get your manicure, how you are so scared of death every six months you get your blood tested to see if one of those poor victims you keep ripping off didn't give you something. So I took samples from the lab and particles of your skin from the beauty parlor. "

"For what?" smith asked again, surprised.

"Tomorrow cops in Detroit will get anonymous letter with the name of the guy who robbed the bank in Chicago. By pure coincidence his blood type and DNA will match the Chicago robber."

"What do I have to do with this?" Smith just kept asking.

"Name of the robber will be Smith," said Mark pulling out of his wallet a photograph. "This is the photo of your friend from four months ago," Mark kept on going. "He never crossed you out as a friend."

The only thing Smith noticed reaching out for the photograph was the gold Rolex on the stranger's hand. Mark got up and started to walk towards exit. When he was by the door Smith shouted: "Thank you!"

Mark turned around and said: "It's never too late to be a human being."

***

Andrzej looked around anxiously; to the left, to the right. He didn't know why he was here. He has never done this before but today something told him to try.

Yes, he thought, *I have to try once. Maybe I will fall in love or she will. I wander why I am doing this? I had never before paid for making love to somebody. I can't believe myself. Maybe I better turn around.*

Instantly though, his mind reacted: *Don't even think about it. You won't turn around. You've had your mind made up and that's it.*

The street was full of "girls" and "boys" looking for adventures as well as money on the street. Not the top shelf-clothed girls walked firmly back and forth down Woodward Avenue. What drives young girls to selling their bodies for money? Maybe some get some kind of a kick out of sleeping around and allowing to be touched all over by strangers for pennies. The better ones do not promenade on the streets but hide in the giant metro, selling themselves for more. Either way it's not about sensations but money. Some say it's an easy way to make it. Maybe it is but one has to have nerves of steel, patience, wit and intelligence. The not-so-clever ones get lost in gutters, raped, with slit throats or doped up. Yet there is clear difference between prostitutes. The ones who do it so they can make more money, dress better etc. – call them "professionals". What about those who aren't so pretty, with stretch marks after giving birth, with no husbands anymore or families to help them? Well, we could call them "warriors". Yeah, this fits them, the women with no way out, who love their kids and aren't afraid to take a punch or two, and be treated like dirt for a few bucks. They fight for their status, for their right to be in this world used up by money. Who are they? What do they want? Do they like to sing or dance? Nobody seems to want to answer that nobody ever will because for a split second we might come to conclusion that we ourselves created civilization that now creates the "warriors". By eliminating poverty we would reduce crime by 50%. It would cost less than up keeping of the prisons, police, courts and lawyers. Nobody thought of it or nobody wants to think about it.

Andrzej suddenly slowed down, drove up to the curb and stopped. He pushed the button and the window went down without a sound.

"Hop in," he said to the girl walking by.

"Me?" The blonde asked.

"Yeah, you. Hop in before some cop shows up and there'll be trouble."

The girl sat in the car looking at Andrzej curiously. He took off.

"Where are you going?" She asked.

"Home," he replied.

"I'm not going home with you!" She screamed. "Stop. I'm leaving."

"What you want me to do, fuck you here on the street?"

"Let's go to a motel."

Andrzej pushed the gas pedal.

"I take fifty bucks for half hour and a hundred for a full hour," she said.

"Ok," he mumbled.

"If you want without a rubber, it's extra fifty."

Andrzej looked with concern.

"You take it without a condom?" He asked surprised.

"Yes."

"How many guys a day do you?"

"On a good day ten."

Andrzej stopped by the motel. Once he got out of the car he came up to the window and asked: "How much per hour?"

"Twenty five bucks," a guy responded from behind the bullet proof window.

"Ok, let's do it."

"Your driver's license," he hears the receptionist's voice.

"I'll show you my driver's license, you moron," Andrzej barked back angrily. The receptionist went silent, took the money and gave Andrzej the key. The girl, once she saw Andrzej with the key, got out of the car now, fixed her skirt and started to follow him. He opened the room door and came in. Nothing but a large bed covered with colorful blanket, an end table, refrigerator and TV set. The girl said "It's cozy in here." Andrzej sat down on the bed.

"Undress," he said.

"Money first," the girl answered.

Andrzej reached to his pocket and whipped out a stack of bills.

"Oh wow!" The girl said, "You are loaded."

Andrzej got a hundred dollar bill without saying a word: "Here, now go and take a shower."

The girls went to the bathroom.

Nasty room in a shady motel with a whore, peak of dreams, Andrzej thought.

The girl came out of the bathroom totally naked. Her long, blonde hair was reaching the breasts which no longer seemed full and perky. Her hips rounded with excess of fat no longer excited. Andrzej was not about to judge her looks. He got up and took off his clothes as well.

"You are so muscular," the girl said.

Silence, as Andrzej said nothing. He grabbed her by the waist line and tucked his face in her hair. The scent of freshness did not match her posture and there was something delicate about this girl. He felt a gentle touch on his member as her hand began its journey through his sack to end up again on his erected penis. This time his hand wandered between her legs. She was wet and her hips swayed in the harmonious resonance of excitement, they fell on the bed. Andrzej kissed her neck passionately and slowly reached her torso. The girl was gasping. Andrzej was ready to enter with full passion then the whole atmosphere was lost. The girls said: "Put the condom on unless you want to pay extra."

Andrzej cooled off momentarily.

"You could have waited until it is all over," he said.

"Oh, no, dear; money first."

"I am not going to give you anything more. Put the condom on," he said mad.

The girl reached to her purse and took out a condom. Skillfully she opened it and grabbed Andrzej's manhood.

"Leave it," he said.

"What is it?" she asked surprised.

"We're not gonna fuck," He announced.

"You don't like me?"

"It's not that," he responded quickly, "Keep the money and put back on the clothes."

The girl complied with his order.

"Do you have any kids?" He asked her.
"Yes."

"How many?"

"Three boys," she responded.

"Nice. How old are you?"

"Twenty seven."

"What shampoo do you use?"

"I don't use shampoo, only unscented soap. Why ask?"

"Because your hair smells like hop, like life."

"Thanks," the girl said, "Nobody has told me that yet."

"I didn't think that anyone has." He reached to his pocket and pulled out two hundred dollars, gave it to the girl.

"Here, get something for the boys."
"Thank you. You're a good man."

Andrzej stood up and pulled the girl towards him. He wanted to kiss her lips but she pulled herself away.

"No, please don't. I don't kiss clients."
"Then whom do you kiss?"

"Those I love," she answered.

Andrzej looked serious.

"What? You're gonna take the money back now, huh?"

"No, I don't take back what I once gave. I just thought that..."

"That what?" She asked.

"That perhaps you could fall in love with me."

"You're a handsome and wealthy man with good heart. But no, I don't love you and I probably never would. Don't be mad, please."

"I'm not. For a moment I simply thought that everyone should just love me simply because of the fact that I am."

* * *

Mark parked the car and looked around. The Arabic neighborhood was full of life. He slowly started off towards the barber shop. He knew this part of town and liked it; maybe because he felt somewhat strange and yet comfortable here.

They're strangers in America too, he thought; speak their own language because it helps them to remember they are different. English doesn't unite people. It allows for communication but doesn't unite them. After all, we are not all equal, or the same – that would be boring. Politicians try to tell us we are all equal. The global economy, global decisions – all this is said in the name of equality but in fact the main goal is always the profit. Yes, money makes us lose everything that is dear to us, ourselves. Religion helps people to unite but does it help them love? The Muslims think they are different than Christians. Hindu people think they are different than Muslims and so it has been for thousands of years. Instead of love we only deepen our differences. We lost the value of an individual and it's the masses that count. They bamboozle us with "mass equals power" and an individual is just a part of the masses. What an idiotic concept. We learn nothing from the mistakes. It was the great mass of the Third Reich that collapsed. The Soviet Union C*ollapsed. Why? Because somebody wanted for millions of people to think and act the same. Now we are building the European Union and the United States. Nobody drew any conclusion from the past. When I speak* *to a German, I want for him or her to feel that I speak to them and not to a member of the European Union. When I speak do an Arab, I want him or her to feel I speak to them and not to a Muslim. I think they feel the same but are too afraid to open up for the learned fear of God or the President. Wouldn't it be better if...*

His divagations were interrupted by the voice of the barber.

"Good morning there, Mr. Mark."

"Good morning, he returned the greeting.

"So nice of you to come and see us again. Please, take a seat. The usual?"

"Oh yes, Mark answered.

The barber skillfully wrapped the apron towel around Mark's neck.

"What's new in the great big world? He stirred up the small talk.

"Not a whole lot; just work and more things to do."

"Oh yes, the barber continued, "But whenever I see you I always hope to hear something wise. There is always this calm and optimism beaming off of you. You always smile and need comes, you are always there to help the ordinary folks."

"I am an ordinary guy myself, Mark responded, "I like music and I like to dance, making love to women. My smile it is just a representation of my approach to life. People often forget who they are and where they are heading. The worry over things that are yet to be. They're preoccupied with thinking about tomorrow not paying attention to what is there now, or dwell on things of the past in fear about tomorrow thus missing out on today. For me what matters if the today because this is what I am going through at the moment. Worrying about tomorrow will not have an impact on what tomorrow brings.

"How so? It's good to preplan things." the barber said puzzled.

"Not at all. Planning is illusionary and if you want to preplan everything you will put limits on yourself."

"But why?" The barber kept asking.

"Because preplanning your future you think about the past and that's what is confusing."

"How so? It is good to draw conclusions so we can avoid repeating the same mistakes."

"It is a half-truth but today you are not the same person anymore that you were yesterday. If you continue taking up perspective as if you were still a twenty years old and keep being scared of making the mistakes you had made when you were, in fact twenty years old, then you will not progress at all at anything."

"Hmm, that is interesting, the barber said. To what to do in order...not to plan?"

"You need to live the today, find the harmony of life and love thyself."

"But the bills still have to be paid but who is going to pay them for me?" The barber kept asking.

"Ah, that's it," Mark smiled. "People have learned to think we are what we have; I am what I do; I am what people see me as;. I believe in God. Truly we just don't know who we are. We don't know when we are happy."

"Well, so when are we happy?"

"I can't answer that. You have to find an answer of your own."

"How do I look for one? The barber asked.

"Get rid of the past. Don't think about what was. Don't think about what will be and just focus on today. Learn to enjoy the present day and do not push away problems for they will always be nearby. Try to accept them and once you learn to see them at a distance, they will not seem so terrifying. I can tell you a story, if you want."

"Well, sure I do, the barber said eagerly.

Mark straightened his posture and once comfortable began to talk.

"Long, long time ago, somewhere in the rocky mountain tops three wise men met

They met so they could chat about the meaning of life. So they were sitting like that around the bonfire when suddenly a nymph from space arrived and appeared in front of them. She brought three pitchers with her with some drink in it called life. She offered it to the first wise man, to have a bit of life but he declined. Life is disgusting. I'm not gonna drink it, he said. She offered the second pitcher to the next one but he, in fear of bitterness of life, only had a sip and once drank it he got shakes and chills. The nymph then came up to the third wise man offering him what she had offered to the previous two. This time the man grabbed all three pitchers and drank all of their content to the bottom. Once he finished the third and last one he stood up, began to dance and sing laughing at the same time passionately. ?hat happened to you? The other wise men asked. ? Don't know, he answered them dancing, but I like what's been happening to me and I don't want for it to stop."

Mark paused with his story and the barber kept on cutting the hair in silence.

"And, what happened next?" He asked after a moment.

"That's it, Mark replied."

"That's the end?" The barber was surprised, "here is the moral of the story?"

"You come up with your own moral" Mark said.

"Help me, please", the barber asked somewhat embarrassed.

"Ok, well the moral of the story could be this: we cannot take life as if it were fruits on the market you pick and

choose which ones you like and which ones to throw away as rotten. Life is to be taken as it is, with all its good and bad. Once you mix it all up, this is when we can begin to dance and sing and be happy to be alive. There are no more sincere tears than the tears of sadness and smiles deeper than the one of love. Let's allow life to surprise us and stop trying to defend ourselves from it."
That sounds nice, the barber started, but…"

"There is no *but* Mark cut him off, you just have to take life as it is and that's what is fascinating. Don't rely on reason, learn spontaneity and be driven by heart. Leave reason alone for, contrary to what we might think, it is not our friend. Reason remembers yesterday and plans the future based on that memory but it doesn't know love and what the heart feels. Reason is a machine which ought to work for you and not the other way around. Remember that. Let the reason pay your bills while you sing and dance, and enjoy life."

"I'm finished", the barber said.

"Finished what?" Mark asked.

"The haircut", the barber replied.

"Ah", Mark awoke.

"Your hair always comes out nice after the cut", the barber said.

"Oh, stop it", Mark answered with a smile. "It came out nice because you are just very good at what you do and that's all there's to it."

The barber smiled as well.

"You're right. I am good."

"See, isn't it great to know you are good at things?"

"It certainly is."

"You do it every day and every guy you cut the hair off is always pleased. How many clients do you get daily, would you say?"

"About ten."

"How many years have you been doing this?"

"Around fifteen years."

"Ten guys a day for fifteen years gives you about forty thousand happy people. I do not think there is a politician in the world who could compete with you when it comes to satisfying the people."

"Thank you very much. I have never thought of it this way."

"You see how much good you have done in life?"

"Now I do."

"You take care," Mark said upon leaving.

He left the barber shop and walked towards the parking lot. He fixed the gold Rolex on his wrist.

Isn't that a great feeling to help people in feeling that they matter? He thought. *Smile on this barber's face put me in excellent mood. Life is great and people are wonderful. It is so good to live in the world full of surprises and goodness. I think I will do one more deed...*

He opened the door to his car and sat down, started the engine, picked up a newspaper that was on the other seat, looked at the front page and read the headline 'A 7-year old Girl Raped. Cops Looking For Suspect."

Yeah, Mark thought. *Some people just don't get what's right and what's wrong. You can't just praise everyone. Some need to be reminded what's good and what's evil.*

He put the paper down and grabbed the steering wheel. The car started off with the squeal of tires.

It was a beautiful day, sunny, and the Arabic neighborhood was beaming with life. This Sun shines for every day for every one of us. It makes it possible for us to live, to enjoy the flowers blooming and the rain falling. It makes the snow shine warming up the hearts. Sun is good and only someone completely soulless can turn this beautiful day into a nightmare of darkness and rape. Why, why?

Music is the greatest achievement of our civilization. From the very first steps humanity has made, music has been its everlasting company. Why music? It gathers together everything that's beautiful and makes it into the perfect harmony. Like the human body is made up of hundreds or thousands, it works together in the rhythm of life. Let's look even further; let's see the world that surrounds us. The trees, animals, stars on the sky and waves of the

ocean all is put together in this great harmony. Once we leave the Earth atmosphere, we wind up in Cosmos. The Earth spins around its own ax while spinning around the Sun. All this is a part of the galaxy. The Solar System constantly travels, remains in motion and there is not a day when it is stagnant. We are in constant motion. The music that we feel every day is a representation of our destiny. Yes, this is the secret of our existence; constant energy and constant motion.
Andrzej was sitting on the balcony smoking a cigar. He thought about the world and his place in this harmonious giant.

Women, he thought. What do I want from the women? Everything I do, I do for women. Starting with mom I wanted to please her with my walk, my talk. Then I moved to girl-friends in school I wanted to show them how well I swim, play soccer. And then the first girlfriend I told her stories to prove how smart and intelligent I was. There was the first kiss on the lips, the first touch of breasts and finally the first act, which showed me that our lives are in constant motion and in order to attain orgasm we have to be in motion as well. Now, after all these years, I realize that everything I do, I do for women. Funny. So what do I want from a woman? I think just one thing he thought I expect harmony. Yes, she has to become a part of my life music. A man is a living musical note. There are no two notes, just one. Yes, everyone is of its own kind and only proper connection of the notes can make up for music. Some tunes are sad while others joyous but all either way they are all melodies and as such cannot called good or bad just because they are sad or joyous. As long as the notes fit and stay in harmony the melody lasts. Today I can make love to a blonde, tomorrow to a brunette,

And the day after with a tall one while later on with a shorty and as long as her note fits my turn and vice versa, the song is on. There are long and short songs and there are also improvisations. There is blues and jazz as well as the never-ending symphonies. As long as there is rhythm and harmony, everything is in order and there is no need to damage anything. There are no words in music about why this isn't allowed, what's due and what's forbidden. Once we start using those terms our melody is no longer a melody.   We lose the rhythm and we lose harmony. There is no more music only our empty sounds. *Damn*, Andrzej thought, *it all makes sense. Asking questions makes people lie. Especially when there is a question that cannot be answered. Is there love? I think so but how to describe it? Is there betrayal? I don't think there is, for what is a betrayal? Is it some detour from commonly accepted norms? Is it a break from a promise? We cannot promise anyone anything, for we do not control our melody of life. Just because I played in some other melody doesn't mean I no longer fit the old one. I am still the "C" note and nothing changed here. I am still the same note, myself, and I don't fit a particular melody I can be replaced with a different note. To heck with this thinking,* he got mad, *makes me tired. The truth is that if I don't sleep with the girl, I can't say anything about her. I have to get to know her body first. How can one write music without knowing the value and sound of a tune? One cannot think about working on the soul when they are not happy with their body. First – body, then the soul. If I want her body then I will look for her soul, never the other way around.*

Sick and hungry people do not spend time on thinking. Hunger and desire for sex do not go in harmony with meditations. We will never achieve harmony unless we b lance out the physical and intellectual. How can priests meditate when most likely their thought wander between beautiful and full breasts of a woman? How can you love another if you yourself do not know yourself, are hungry and thirsty, and don't love thy own self? Yes, our whole life we do everything for women. They are the ones who built the pyramids and the Eiffel tower. They swam through Atlantic and conquered the South Pole. Who is a man in light of those beautiful eyes of a woman, her juicy breasts and moist vagina? This is our harmony of life and let's not try to stop it. If we do, we take away from our life what's most important, freedom. Enough of this, Andrzej concluded.

He stood up, put down the cigar and finished his coffee.

I'll get out for a while somewhere, get down in a club or something, he thought.

He looked through his closet, put on black pants, white shirt un-tucked, put on the shoes and energetically went down to the garage where the silver Corvette awaited him. He sat in it and started off. With average speed he ran down the streets enjoying the breeze. After a few minutes he pulled up at the club's parking lot. On the roof of a silver neon announced "Excalibur." He drove up to the front door. A young guy in white shirt and red jacket came up and open the car's door.

"Welcome," the guy said.

Andrzej got out of the car, reached to his packet and pulled out a bunch of bills in quest for some 20 dollars but he could not find it for a while.

Oh be darn, only fifties and hundreds, he thought. Finally he found a twenty dollar bill, gave it to the youngster and said:

"Park somewhere up front."

The guy answered with a smile:

"Of course, sir Andrzej. For a twenty I would sleep in this car."

"You better get some flowers for your girl," Andrzej replied.

"Sure thing."

Andrzej walked into the club where at the front, behind the desk, a pretty girl was sitting. Once she saw Andrzej, she stood up and reached out with her hand.

"He," she said.

"Hi there," he replied.

"You promised you would call."

"I was busy," Andrzej said.

"Do you still want to see me?" The girl asked.

"Yes."

"When?"

"I'm not sure."

"Don't think I will sit my whole life at home waiting for your phone call."

"I've never expected that."

"Is this it then? Finish?"

"Finish of what?"

"Of us knowing each other."

"There is no finish. I know you and always will know you. I like you a lot and why would you want me to forget you?"

"You're so strange and I just can't understand you."

"Don't try so hard. Maybe someday we will play our music again."

"What music?"

"Doesn't' matter. Don't listen to me."

"Ok, well do you want your usual VIP table?"

"No, I'll sit at the bar tonight."

"Whatever you want," the girl said and added, "Have fun."

"Thanks."

Andrzej sat at the bar where wood and granite suggested prosperity and wealth. DJ played mellow tunes and laser lights were full of creative figures.

"What can I get you?" The bartender asked.

"Orange juice."

The bartender skillfully opened up a can, poured the juice and placed in front of Andrzej.

"Ten dollars."

Andrzej got a fifty dollar bill and passed it to the guy: "Get a drink for that girl to," he pointed at a brunette sitting nearby, "And keep the change."

"You got it," the bartender answered and gave the girl the drink. She raised the glass as if toasting towards Andrzej and said:

"Thank you."

"You're welcome," he replied.

"You're fast."

"Life's too short."

"My name is Tina."

Andrzej stood up and walked up to her.

"I am Andrzej."

"Take a seat," the girl pointed at the chai by her. Andrzej sat down.

"Do you come here often?" Tina asked.

"I guess. I don't count."

"You have nice hands," she continued.

"And you have pretty eyes, blue?"

"Yes."

"Do you like to sing?" Andrzej asked.

"Sometimes."

"Come on, let's dance. I like this song. Would you sing for me?"

"I can try."

They got up and started off towards the dance floor. They looked great together, stood on the floor. Andrzej grabbed her hand and then gently held her at her waist. She placed her hand on his arm and brushed his hair with her fingers. Then she had her lip by his ear and nibbled it gently. He didn't react. She started humming to his ear and they swayed away on the dance floor without saying anything. They didn't want to interfere with the tune.

***

"I'd like to call my attorney," the prisoner said.

"Shut up," the guard responded.

"What do you mean?!" Inmate was yelling, "I am entitled to it! It's my right!"

"You know what you're entitled to?" The guard asked.

"What?"

"A bullet to your head, you punk."

"Watch your mouth. You'll pay for it."

"No, you'll be the one paying - for raping that girl you'll get a decent sentence."

"I admitted to but I didn't want to!"

"So what you're saying? Somebody forced you to rape and beat someone up?"

"No, it's my alter ego. I have no control in moments like this."

"So we should let you go and wait for you to rape another child somewhere, huh?"

"You have to give me a chance. I will get help – get treatment."

"You already got treatment and what?"

"It wasn't enough!"

"How long do you think you will be getting treatments? Your whole life, perhaps?"

"Yes, if that's what it takes."

"And what about those kids you rape? Somehow they will make it alright?"

"Make it alright? You have no clue what you're talking about. A child like that is a treasure, innocent and open for the world. They want to learn about everything around them, enjoy life, laugh and dance. Kids have the spark in their eyes. It's this spark that we need to cherish and protect. It is almighty. This spark is our god. You've killed this spark."

"Watch what you're saying. Now let me call my lawyer."

"Alright," the guard said and walked up to the cell. He opened the door.

"Go in front and I'll follow."

"Ok," the inmate responded.

They walked in silence. When passing other cells, inmates were walking up to the bars, reaching their fists in silence, clenched, with thumbs down.

"What are they doing?" The prisoner asked.

"How do I know?" The guard answered.

The delinquent came up to the phone and dialed the number anxiously.

"Law offices," he heard on the other end.

"I'd like to speak with Mr. Washington."

"Who is asking?"

"Gary Smith."

"One moment, please."

Music was playing in the background and Smith was nervously thumping with his foot. The guard stood at the distance talking with other inmates. They laughed and joked around. It upset him: *They act as if nothing was happening, as if they were free and meanwhile they will be sentenced soon just like me. Some are here for serious crimes and yet they feel like joking. Here, this one in 5 – Murder and attempt. He will get a life, no question. Smile, you idiot. We'll see if you laugh tomorrow.*

"Hello," the voice on the phone shook Smith and he instantly regained focus.

"Mr. Washington, it's Gary Smith. Please get me out of here, get a bond or something."

"It's not that simple as you may think. What you are there for makes you danger to the society and the judge will not let you out until the trial."

"I'm not a murderer, didn't kill anyone."

"Well and what do you think you did?"

"I raped that one because she looked eighteen, had those panties and skirt on like that... It is her parents' fault – letting her dress like this. She got me excited and I couldn't control myself. Little whores – they do that on purpose."

"Don't full me here, Smith, and tell me you can't tell the difference between a child and an adult. It isn't parents' fault so stop the blame game."

"Well, whatever and wherever the fault, you are the one to find the guilty one."

"Looks like it is you."

"Me? I am paying you to find the guilty one, like could be my father who beat me or mother who didn't love me. It can be school where teachers didn't try hard enough to teach me something. It can be the whole world that would not accept me as long as it isn't me. I don't belong here, to prison. Make me insane and I'll go to the nuthouse but don't let me go to prison."

"Man, what kind of nonsense is that? You had everything planned, had her photos at home, her school schedule so don't give me this she got you excited with her looks and that this was the first time you saw her."

"What shall we do?"

"Plead guilty and seek a deal."

"Are you crazy?"

"Hey, watch what you're saying."

"Watch what I'm saying? I don't give a shit what I'm saying. You must get me out of here!"

"I got you out the first time, when you assaulted that boy, remember?"

"He wanted it!"

"Stop it! Stop this nonsense now! Start taking some responsibility for your actions. Maybe if you do some time, it will put your marbles together."

"You don't want to help me!"

"You can't help somebody who doesn't seek help."

"But I did go to hospitals, met with psychologists!"

"So what? You did it again – raped a child."

"I had to; she was so beautiful, so pure."

"Enough of this conversation!" the guard yelled.

"I have to go," Smith said over the phone.

"Go, think about what I said and if you refuse the guilty plea I am not taking your case."

"Whatever! You thief!" Smith exploded, "I'll find another lawyer that will get me out of here!"

"I see you have made the decision on your own. Good luck."

Attorney on the other end put down the phone leaving Smith in disbelief.

"Hello. Hello!" He kept screaming.

The guard came up to him from behind and put his hand on his shoulder.

"Back to the cell, you jerk."

"Leave me, you..." but he didn't finish the sentence as he felt the burning pain in his legs. The guard smacked him with the rubber baton across the legs.

Smith fell on the ground. The guard grabbed him by the shirt and dragged to his cell accompanied by laughter and whistle of other inmates.

By the evening the small local prison began to fill up like never before. There were youths for bar brawls, disorderly conducts, reckless driving and so on, to the point that in cells designed for two people there were five or six. The guard, somewhat embarrassed, called the sergeant for orders.

"Sorry to bother you but we're busy here like never before. I have twenty inmates and five cells. What shall I do?"

"The ones who got there for something minor – keep them together and don't mix with the repeats," the answer was.

"Yes, sir!" The guard responded and started off towards the cells.

"Hey, Smith! I have to empty this cell and move you to 5."

"I don't wanna go to 5. I want to be alone."

"No other option. I have to move you. That's the order I got."

"I don't want to! No!" Smith yelled.

The guard reached for the baton and Smith got quiet, starting off towards cell number 5.

The whole place was loud now. The young ones yelled at each other, blaming for bar fights. The older ones were yelling back at them to be quiet. At 10 p.m. The place got dark as the lights went out. The situation loosened up and things got quieter. The guard, tired now, sat down and watched some TV in his little room. Two miles away from the prison in the nearby bar the fun was still on. Young crowd danced and played pool. It would be nothing unusual if it were not for the fact that only one guy was paying for it all. He sat to the sides and didn't drink any liquor surrounded by a group of young people who kept him company smiling. Few things could be picked up from their conversations: "I would let them lock me up for five hundred bucks," "And I would maybe even agree to three hundred." The stranger stood up and began to say his farewells.

"Not necessary anymore, guys – we send about twenty guys to the can. They will be out tomorrow and they will be just fine."

"Tell us, why do you do this?" The youngsters kept asking.

"I do this because I like young people and by helping me you also helped a little, seven year old girl."

"Oh yeah? What girl?"

"It is a complicated story and you would not be interested. I thank you though. I knew I could count on youths."

"You're strange," the crowd concluded, "Despite the Rolex on your hand and bunch of money in your pocket you're not full of yourself. You're like one of us."

"Well, thanks once more," the strange man responded and left the bar.

It was about 2 a.m. and the prison was deeply in sleep. Stench of alcohol traveled around the cells and the guard, tired himself, left his little room, looked at the watch and proceeded along the cells.

Once he got to cell 5 he stopped speechless. Smith's body was dangling as the white sheet wrapped around his neck was attached to the ceiling light fixture. The guard looked at the other prisoner who just kept laying down on his bed, staring at the cadaver.

"What happened?" The guard asked.

"What do you mean? He hung himself."

"Hung himself?"

"What, you think I did it?"

"Yeah, as the matter of fact. Where did that giant bruise on his cheek come from? You did him good to the point he lost conscience and then you hang him."

The prisoner sat on his bunk and said:

"Well, it could have been totally differently. When Smith finished talking to his attorney he was so shocked he got insane, got ahold of your baton and you had no choice – had to disarm him. You punched him. Then he fell and you dragged him into my cell."

"Hmm," the guard mumbled, "All other prisoners saw what happened."

"Exactly! They all saw how he got ahold of your baton and you just had no choice," the prisoner continued.

"Why did you do this?" You already have murder charges, face life in prison. Makes no difference to you if you do time for one or two."

"You're right," the prisoner responded, "It may not make a difference to you but it does to me. The one that I shot – I did so because I had to. If I didn't most likely he would have killed me. This is how the life of most criminals like myself ends. But the one dangling here is a chance for both you and me. He got what he deserved. You will still be the same man you were and if you accept my account of what happened you will let me go back to the normal world, the world which has no place for me anymore. Even though we stand on the opposite sides of the bars, for a brief moment we will be on one side together – the right side."

"There is something to it," the guard kept thinking out loud, "Out of the blue all these prisoners here. Somebody is watching over us. But what warranty do I have?"

"You don't need warranty if you are at pair with good."

"Damn you," the guard said, "call me crazy but I will do what you're asking."

When the guard finished he looked at the prisoner and suddenly felt overpowering relief. He felt happy as the spark appeared in the inmate's eye. It was a spark of freedom.

* * *

Andrzej was no longer asleep. He put his head on his palm and just stared. Full hair was flowing gently down her arms. She was lying across; her breasts moving to the rhythm of the breath. He gently removed the sheet and now saw her full, nude. No pubic hair – he liked it. *Nice tan*, he thought. He could not stop himself; placed his hand on her stomach and felt her breathe. Slowly he moved his hand up her hips. She moved, as if startled. He stopped for a moment. He waited and then moved from the hips, along her legs to the feet. She moved again. He waited. He started moving again towards her hips, brushing against her vagina as she moved again and he, once more, paused. After a split moment again he touched her hips, her stomach, reaching for her breast – hardened now with anxiously perky nipples. He put is head down, put one nipple in his mouth and instantly felt blood storming inside his head. He lifted his head up and started to sniff her hair. With his hand on her crotch he was indulging in the scent of her hair. She shook but he did not pay attention now. He felt moisture on his finger and reached deeper. Her vagina was wet. He was not interrupting this journey now, deeper and deeper. She opened her eyes.

"You're here," she said.

"I am," he quietly responded.

"I had a dream that you were gone."

"I am here, Tina, I'm here," he whispered.

"I want you," she said reaching for his member.

He shook from excitement and she gently spread out her legs. Their lips met now in a passionate kiss. Gently she guided his penis inside her vagina as they dwelled in the kiss. She moved her hips gently. He started his dance as she kept up with her hips. They started slowly, picking up the pace. After a moment they found each other's rhythm. There was no

More of him or her. They were only together. The music began. They just continued joined in this life dance throughout the ages or through a brief moment only. Did that really matter? They were together and that's what mattered. When hot lava exploded in her burning insides she moaned. Motion weakened until they stopped completely. They still stayed in the kiss. Andrzej stopped and lifted his head up. She stared right in his eyes. Silence. And so they stayed, staring at each other throughout the ages or through a brief moment only. Who cared? They were together and that's what mattered.

Andrzej wanted to say something but she put her finger on his lips.

"Hush," she whispered, "I don't want to lose this."

He got quiet and just looked in her eyes. He felt happy; didn't have to think, to react, to do anything. This moment had something unrepeatable, something beyond description.

This is love, he thought.

The tranquility of this paradise was suddenly interrupted by the sound of the phone.

"Oh no!" Andrzej screamed. "What does everyone want from me? It is Sunday after all. Can't I be left alone?"

He lazily got off the bed and came up to the phone.

"Hello?" He said.

"Hi Andrzej," sounded on the other end.

"What do you want?" Andrzej asked carelessly.

"I am sorry to bother you but this is important."

"Go ahead. I'm listening."

"There is an opportunity to make a few bucks."

"Go on, don't stop."

"Ok, there is a nice building to be taken in Southfield. The guy is going bankrupt and the building will be auctioned in three weeks. We only have three weeks.

"Ok but three weeks to do what?"

"You have to find some loser with good credit. I have a buddy. He will appraise this building for 2.2 million. The owner doesn't want anything, just to pay off what he owes to the bank."

"How much does he owe?"

"Eight hundred thousand."

"Ok, go on."

"Let's find somebody to get a loan for 2.2 million. The cash goes to the owner. He pays off the bank and there is 1.4 million left. He gives the cash to us. We give ten grand to the loser who played the role and there is one million three hundred and ninety thousand left. This is our pay out. We give my buddy fifty for the appraisal, another fifty to the banker who grants the loan. One million two hundred and ninety thousand left. JJ takes two hundred ninety thousand and we have a million!

"How do we lauder the cash?"

"Aren't you curious? Just be happy and jump instead of asking some questions."

"It's important. I don't want to go to the can for half a million."

"Ok, ok then. There is a company in Hawaii that will transfer the money to a bank in Argentina. We take the vacation and cash in. Deal?"

"Deal," Andrzej said with a smile, "Everything will be ready by Wednesday."

"I knew you would like it. You never disappoint, Andrzej."

"Ok then, till Wednesday."

Andrzej put down the phone and went back to the bedroom.

"Who was that?" Tina asked.

"A co-worker."

"He couldn't wait till Monday?"

"No."

"So what now?" She asked.

Andrzej jumped right back into bed and pulled her towards him in embrace.

"It was a great night," he said.

"Night and morning," she replied, "Nobody excites me like you."

"The way you tempt. One look at you and I can feel my blood boiling."

She laughed.

"I'm glad you see me like this. You will stay with me for a while."

"I will."

"For how long?"

"Don't ask questions, please. There are no answers."

"Ok, ok but it would be nice to know just for how long will I keep making your blood boil?"

"Here you go again, asking those questions."

"It isn't a question. It's a wish."

"You see, I'd like to be with you for infinity; not till death for that would be too easy. I'd like to have you for infinity."

"Have me then. I won't run."

"It's not about that. I have to be sure that I want you not just so I can sleep with you and enjoy your body. I would like to give you something that would make us both proud, so that our relationship is based on being separate and yet still together, and thus we would be happy in this peculiar separation."

"It's hard to understand you, my dreamer – you."

"These are not dreams. It's a chase."

"A chase? After what?"

"After love, true love, based on freedom."

"It is really hard to understand it."

"I know. I don't get it myself but I know that once this true love comes, I'll recognize it."

"Would you like to have children?"

"Yes but what would I offer them?"

"That's exactly it – what?" She repeated.

"Look at me and tell me who I am."

"I've known you since yesterday. What can I say?"

"Just try."

"You are handsome. You have money and you make love passionately, giving it 100 percent. You are well-read. You are confident but you like to be pampered, like a child."

"Not bad, not at all. Go on."

"You are a good man, kindhearted. Perhaps what you've said about me is true but what is it really – the truth? A silly combo of circumstances? An event true for today can be something false tomorrow. What is true today remains such for you and me. If we share our truth with others it may turn out we've lied. People like to judge us for what we do."

"Yes. You are right," Tina interjected.

"When people love each other, it shows."

"That's why people believe when they know people love."

"Hey," Andrzej cut in suddenly.

"What did you see?"

"Darling, what's out there is emptiness, nothing. Just because people kiss, embrace and express love to one another – this is not love just yet."

"Then what is?"

"It is a learned set of behaviors."

"Nonsense! That's love, exactly."

"No, I disagree."

"So what's love, Mr. Smarty?"

"Love is the abbey, the highest level of human maturity. It's a feeling experienced by one person alone. When he or she loves, anything is possible; problems disappear as do the obstacles. You are the only one who can feel it and without ability to tell about it. Love knows no fear and no boundaries for possibilities. You know those old tales? In every one of them, no matter what its origin, there is the main theme: a boy wants a girl or a girl wants a boy. Family, whole society usually is against it, that love of theirs. The causes may vary: age, wealth, beauty. Yet the main character pays no attention to any of it. He or she follows the goal as if lost marbles. Mountains are flipped upside down and water gets turned into wine, jugnle gets conquered and dragon loses battles. Everyone around knows they should never accomplish what they desire because common sense and laws of physics, chemistry and whatever are all against them succeeding. But they keep paying no attention to that and just keep fighting the windmills. In fairy tales they usually ultimately win. In our lives we fear love. We pretend we love. In truth though, we're afraid of it. So, we kiss each other, embrace and tell how much we love each other but the true love is not there."

Tina listened intrigued. After a brief moment, said:

"What do you want, dreamer you?"

"I want to love without fear, feel the power that knows no boundaries and no limitations of reason."

"Your mother," Tina asked, "Do you love her?"

"I know where you're going with this," Andrzej answered, "You want me to lie again, say that I love her. In reality, think; mother and father gave me life, cared for me and nurtured. I cherish this and respect them for it. I am glad they are here and can share their joys and their sorrows. I can't say I love them because they do not give me that power that love is supposed to give. Maybe it is just a matter of language and perhaps there should be a word added to vocabulary that would reflect our feelings towards parents, siblings and friends. But it is not love, certainly."

"Seems you could never love me," Tina said.

"That depends on you and not on me at all," Andrzej answered. "Do you love me?"

"To love you one would have to learn how," Tina answered jocularly.

"I guess you could say that but in truth, it's not the matter of learning."

"Then what?"

"It's that of understanding."

"Understanding of what?"

"Of yourself. Do not expect anything from me. Just look at yourself and when the moment comes when you're ready to move mountains, you will love me then."

"And what about you?"

"And I will remain the same, unchangeable."

"When will you love?"

"Let's be together and if we keep giving each other the energy to create, then we will never be apart."

"What about the wedding?"

"A wedding? You want me to start lying all over again?"

"But you said there was no truth and there was no lie."

"Yes. This is why I don't want a wedding. The wedding vows make you responsible. Even when we stop giving each other this magical energy, we still remain tied by the fake alliance. There would be no love anymore and hatred would arrive."

"I won't think about that anymore – the love. Come here; I want to have you inside me and feel how you're alive, crazy you. I want you now, right away and whether or not I love you makes no difference."

"That was a cool thing to say. It makes sense. I want you as well, now, right away."

They embraced each other and deep kiss disarmed the situation. They kissed passionately and their energy was out there to work. Is this moment going to survive tomorrow? Does it matter? Let's just live it. Hush...Hush...

*　*　*

Mark drove a solid ride while the traffic was picking up. The number of lanes increased; two, three and now five while the number of cars around, instead of loosening up, kept rising as well. Everyone slows down at once just to pick up the speed the moment after.
This is it, Chicago. Mark thought. He was on West bound I-94 as he saw the familiar exit – Monroe St. He took right and solon was above the freeway already going towards the lake along with thousands of people moving around the giant moloch. Cars running to places known only to them with the sounds of horns of those inpatient with the slowly moving ones. He now drove slowly. He liked this time. Upon seeing the lake he began to dream. *This water, the buildings...Nature. Civilization, He* thought. *Everything we have achieved; concrete, steel, and glass – all this right here at the shore of this great lake. It sits here so self-assured, untouchable and unmoved by anything. The only power is in the nature. The skyscrapers and colorful streets are all great but mean nothing in comparison to this stoic force.   This lake captures people and ships and yet when we look at it we love it for its power and decisiveness. Is there that force for which we long for the entire life of ours? Is this the realization of our dreams of the Almighty One? We want to be strong, have the incredible power of dictating to the world how and what. Once the world turns its back on us is when we turn too God for help. The lake asks for no help but awaits us and accepts whatever the challenge anyone wants to throw at it. It has no opinion on the burning issues but*

eliminates the weak ones, the ones with no character and ones blinded by deceit. I like this lake. I like the nature. I also like love, sex and friendship. I like what's simple and requires no interpretation.

I like evil and good. There is no evil or good just as there is no truth or lie. There only is life and no death. Mark stopped here with his divagations and drove up to a hotel. "Drake" Hotel is one of the best in Chicago. A smiley-faced boy ran up to the car and got the door.

"Welcome to Chicago," he said.

"Ah, thank you. What's new?" Mark answered.

"Everything's alright. We're alive and happy."

"That's a good thing. Boy, enjoy life when you can."

Mark entered the lobby and quickly passed the stairs finding himself in a large hall with gorgeous, several feet tall flower bouquets. He came up to the front desk where an Arabic woman with a smile asked him:

"How can I help you?"

"I have a room reservation; fourth floor, view on the lake. Here is my number," he showed.

The Arabic woman typed the numbers on the keyboard and soon after gave Mark the keys.

"Enjoy your stay," she said.

Mark asked her "Where are you from?"

"I am from Syria" she replied.

"Beautiful country. Do you believe in God?"

"Yes," somewhat shyly but she answered, "In my God."

"And what God is that?"

"Goodness and a smile," she said.

"Wow, is that something," Mark smiled, "I thought all Arabs believe in Allah."

"Perhaps if they would not be teaching us about Allah from the very early age, we would have found him ourselves. There is no Allah and perhaps never has been. I like to believe in what I see. Goodness and a smile are very likeable and with us every day. Why to believe in something that is strange and foreign to me? And you, do you believe in God?"

Mark thought for a while.

"I don't believe in any God but after talking to you I may have a chance to change my mind."
"Oh, yes?" The Arabic woman said with a smile again.

"Yes, Miss. Maybe the time has come to listen to the youths as opposed to living the past."

"You believed in me?"

"Yes dear. I myself find it surprising but yes, I believed in you."

He turned around and followed to the elevator.

The hotel room was of average size with large queen or king size bed, neatly made. Delicate curtains separated the room from the window behind which the lake shined. Mark came up to the telephone and dialed a number. After a brief moment he heard the voice on the other end: "Hello."

"Is this Mr. Larson?"

"Yes, it is." The voice on the other end confirmed.

"Good evening. I am a friend of your parents."

"What do you want?!" Larson yelled.

"I would like to talk to you about your parents."

"There is nothing to talk about!"

"Oh, yes." Mark said with disappointment. "You forged signatures of your parents on the estate sale papers. They had lived in it for twenty five years. Once you acquired the estate you threw them out to live in some shelter where they are till today. You took all of their savings and sent them to live a long and humiliating vegetation. How they did you wrong?"

Silence occurred on the other end as Larson kept quiet.

"It is hard to admit that you are a piece of garbage, isn't it?"

"I have nothing to say," Larson said. "Talk to my lawyer."

"I did not come here to talk to your lawyer."

"So why did you come here, then?"
"I am asking that you return to your parents everything you have taken away from them; the house, the money. Later you will invite them to a dinner and politely apologize for everything. I am sure they will forgive you."

"You're insane. I had taken a loan on the house and the money is lost already. Their savings are long gone 'with the wind'. I have nothing."

"They had worked for this house for twenty five years," Mark said.

"So what? They didn't need that money anyway."

"Ah," Mark sighed,"and how do you figure that they didn't need it anyway?"

"What do old people need the money for?"

"They need it, you moron, so that they can give it to their kids but voluntarily."

"Don't call me moron!"

"Oh, I'm sorry, you idiot." Mark said.

"You are insulting me. I am going to hang up."

"You won't. You're already scared, you punk. You have time till tomorrow to make up your mind."

"Tomorrow?" Larson yelled. "I have to think it through."

"You have time till tomorrow," Mark said firmly.

"What if I don't give them the money back?"

"You will be carrying out consequences of your dumb decisions."

"What consequences?"

"I'm not sure. What sentence would you give yourself for what you had done?"

"I didn't do anything!"

"Stop with this nonsense. We're not in court. Nobody is listening to you. You are all alone, pal."

"I didn't do anything. Leave me alone or I will call police."

"If you do not make up your mind by tomorrow noon, there will be consequences."

"OK, ok. If I change my mind, how should I contact you?"

"You don't have to contact me. What for? Go to your parents, apologize, return the money and be the man. What do you need me for?"

"They've sent you?"

"Nobody has sent me you rat. Tomorrow at noon. Remember."

Mark hang up. *What a piece of nothing,* he thought.

He picked up the phone again and dialed another number.

"Niki?" He asked.

"Yes."

"Hi. Mark here."

"My sweet, I haven't seen you in years. Where are you?"

"I'm in Chicago."

"Great. Dinner tonight at 9:00?"

"Sounds good. What restaurant?"

"You pick the place and let me know, Bye."

She put the phone down. *Always in a hurry, as usual. 'You pick, you chose, you do'...*He thought. He smiled to himself now.

There is nothing more beautiful in the world than the Chicago street. Small bar and large bar next to each other. One plays jazz while the other one blues. And then there is the Irish tune flowing from the third one. Crowds of people; rich and poor, beggars on the streets. Everything here is melted in one harmony of comfort of civilization. How much is the skyscraper? What about this line of cars? How much is gas that makes it possible for them to move? Millions and millions of dollars up in the air. Power, splendor and poverty. It could have been so differently. Love is everywhere. It's free and no investment needed to reach out from it infinitely. What is stopping us from reaching the highest level of humanity? Why can't we afford love that is free? We are all beggars, slaves of our ignorance. For the thousands of years we have reached nothing of value, nothing! We are but a herd of degenerated liars entrapped in the web of betrayal and lies. This is vegetation. We know how to hate but not how to love.

Chicago is a beautiful city, representing power and splendor. There is no love in Chicago or...maybe there is – behind that corner, on the edge of freedom and infinity. Love is right next to us, right there every day and every night. Let's not be afraid to love. Love knows no boundaries, no obstacles and cannot be bought. Love is free!

Niki was dressed in elegant, black dress. The cut-out in the front emphasized the large shapes. She was tall, slender with blond hair gently falling off over her shoulders. She was looking at Mark with curiosity.

"What are you looking at?" He asked. "I haven't seen you in so long."

"Indeed."

"What's been going on?"

"Nothing new, really; work and family stuff."

"How do you handle all this, Mark?"

"I'm trying as best as I can."

"Your wife has to love you very much."

"Why do you think so?"

"She lets you travel and do all this business."

"That's true. I've never thought about it."

"Sure you haven't. It's us – women who see those things. Guys don't pay attention."

"Thanks for telling me this. Maybe I should be spending more time with the family."

"Don't ask me, Mark."

"Why not?"

"I don't want to be your girl-friend."

Mark got silent for a moment. He looked in her eyes which shined somewhat devilishly.

"Then who do you want to be?" He asked after a moment.

"A woman."

"And what about me?"

"You be the man."

Mark got quiet again.

"Is this a proposition?"

"No, not a proposition," she answered with a smile. "I just simply don't want to be here with you and talk about your wife. I want to spend this evening with a man and not somebody's husband."

"Ok." Mark said.

He stood up from behind the table and came up to Niki, kissed her hand and poured wine into her glass. He sat down and raised his glass.

"To your beautiful eyes and great, sexy wardrobe," he toasted.

"Thank you," she whispered. "Now you're the man."

"Thanks," Mark answered. "I'm curious as to how are you in bed?"

"You'll never know, sweetie. I want you to want me but you'll never taste my body."

"That's reasonable and I can live with that."

"I would want you as well but I prefer to long for."

"Why?"

"I'm afraid that if we spent the night together, the next morning we would no longer have the desire for each other."

Mark was quiet as Niki was drinking slowly. After a brief moment she set aside her glass and said:

"This old bag two tables behind us just keeps staring at you."

Mark looked behind him.

"Eh, you're just imagining this."

"Oh, no I am not." Niki kept on, "I know when a woman stares at a man and when she doesn't."

"Well, maybe I am easy on her eyes."

"No, that's not it. She is dressed modestly and wears very comfortable shoes. She doesn't fit this place. Besides, she sits alone and isn't expecting anyone."

"How do you know?"

"She hasn't looked at her watch once. She is watching over you, Mark."

"Give it a rest." Mark said. "Here, in Chicago?"

"Yes, right here."

"For what reason?"

"I don't know but you should."

Mark got serious.

"Ok," he said, "let's get up and leave. If she follows us that means you are right. If not, you are wrong and lost it..."

"Lost what?"

"A kiss."

"No my dear. You will not get me with a trick."

"Ok, a glass of wine."

"Ok, I agree."

They both got up and started off towards exit. Mark on the way called for the waiter and forced a hundred dollar bill in his hand.

"Keep it. No change needed," he said.

Thy left and walked down the street. The passed a few hundreds of yards and Mark came up to the curb pretending to be calling for a cab. In reality though, he stared deep into the street searching for the strange woman. There she was. He saw her. His heart started to race.

Niki was right, he thought. *She is following me. Could Larson be smarter than I thought?*

"Niki," he said, "take the cab and go home but cruise through the city a bit. You were right. That woman is following me."

"Is it something serious?"

"I'm not sure but I don't want you to be with me. Go home and be careful."

"Mark, I've never seen you this concerned. I feel like I am scared for you!"

"Don't be. Just go home and I will call you later."

Niki waved her hand and the cab instantly appeared by the curb. She sat in it and after a moment stuck her head out and said "Be careful, my man."

"I will be," he answered calmly.

Now we will take care of you, cuter. He thought looking after the stranger.

He himself waved for a cab and once it stopped he got in maintaining the calmness.

"Where to?" the taxi cab driver asked.

"Wait, I will tell you in a minute," Mark said.

He kept looking through the window trying to spot the woman. She stood on the street looking in his direction. After a brief moment a minivan drove by and she got in it.

"Go." Mark said to the driver, "We're heading to the south side."

The driver looked at him embarrassed.

"At this hour? Go South? Are you crazy?"

"Don't freak out. I know where I'm going." Mark said. He reached to his pocket and gave the driver a hundred dollar bill. The man took it, put in his pocket and started to drive. Mark reached for his cell phone and dialed a number.

"Hello," the voice on the other end said.

"Hi, Mark here."

"Good evening Mr. Mark. What can I do for you?"

"I am on Michigan Ave. going south. I will be on the State in ten minutes. In fifteen I will be under the overpass of State and I-94. There is a blue Lumina behind me. Stop them and find out who they are and whom they work for? Keep them for seventeen hours. Send the bill as usual."

"No problem, Mr. Mark. Getting on it."

Mark put the phone down.

"Slow down," he told the driver. He looked behind and the Lumina was still there. *Good*, he thought. He looked at the time showing on his shining Rolex. They were approaching I-94 and drove under the bridge.

"Now, go! Fast!" He yelled.

The taxi cab driver followed the direction and pushed the gas as the tires squeaked. Lumina was now far behind. Mark waited a few seconds.

"Stop!" he yelled again.

The car now stopped. Mark got out and looked in the direction of the bridge. The Lumina never emerged from it. "Good job," he said to himself.

He went back to the taxi.

"Drake Hotel, please."

The driver didn't say anything, just drove away.

Police cars surrounded the marina. Some officers were putting yellow tape in places separating he marina from the parking lot. In the corner, other cops were placing somebody's body into an ambulance. The inspector came up to one of the officers and asked:

"Do you know who this is?"

"Yes, he had his driver's license in his pocket. His name is Larson."

"Did you get ahold of his family yet?"

"Yes, his parents live in a nursing home. They were not particularly affected when I told them their son drowned."

"Why not?"

"They said they had not had any contact with him for a long time."

"How come? Do you have any cues?"

"Nah, but he seems like one of those guys who once had a few cocktails wants to be a ship captain. He slipped and fell in between two boats. He got squashed but really instead of maintaining some cold blood he panicked and that's what did him."

"I'll buy it," the inspector said, "Accident – close the case."

***

"And I want a big house," Tina said.

Andrzej looked at her smiling.

"What do you need a big house for?"

"What do you mean? For us."

"But I don't need a big house. I want a lot of space and the house is a cage."

"You only say this now but if you had a house with library, entertainment room, card room, pool table etc. you would like it."

"No, not at all. All of that can be done in bars, clubs where there are people I don't know and don't have to invite. In the house you can only host your guests and that's it. A guest is not the company; he has to smile and agree with the host. Bar is the place where a complement is the complement and not just a socially appropriate form."

"What are so mad about all of the sudden?" Tina asked angrily.

"You are the one who started with that entire big house?" Andrzej answered.

"Yes, I said it thinking you would like that."

"Why do you talk about things you have no clues about? Why are you assuming I would want a big house? Why not ask: 'Andrzej, would you like a big house?' Then if I said 'yes', you could go on with all them plans. But you only thought if you mention big house Andrzej would get excited right away, right?"

"Right…" Tina whispered now.

"Next time just ask me straight forward instead of making up some false scenarios."

"Fine. I didn't think you would get ticked off like that."

"I didn't get ticked off but look – we spent half an hour trying to explain to each other things that could have been said in two sentences."

"Ok, ok then. What would you like to talk about?"

"About women's lingerie… I would like it if you started paying attention to what you wear."

"Why do you talk like this? You don't like my lingerie?"

"That's not the point. I would like for you to look far more exciting."

"You want me to look like a slut?"

"Yes, if that's how you want to see it. Wearing something exciting doesn't at all mean you look like a slut. You are a very sexy woman and that's all."

"But I don't like this."

"Now you see, we finally are talking about things that are important and that have to do with me and you every day. So why don't you like to dress provocatively?"

"Because it's not my style."

"Then what is your style?"

"The one I have now, normal."

"This is not an answer. It's a statement not supported by anything."

"Casual means just that: casual, just like now."

"Ok, you look and are dressed nicely, have elegant clothes but there is no character to you. Do you think that's normal?"

"Yes, I think so."

"Are you saying you are just like millions of others?"

"Maybe so."

"Then what am I doing with you. Why am I here, with you instead of with somebody who isn't a part of this multi-million group of 'normal'' ones?"

"I don't know but this conversation makes me tired."

"It makes you tired… But we are talking about us, not about some strangers."

"I know, but it does."

"So what, we're going to talk about a big house and a large bunch of kids?"

"Sounds more dignifying to me."

"Dignifying… Empty shack full of kids, that's dignifying to you?"

"Yes."

Andrzej lit up a cigar.

"You can't smoke in here," Tina said.

"Do you own this place?"

"No."

"So why do you say I cannot smoke here?"

"Because that's what the signs on walls say."

"Yes, the signs say 'Andrzej cannot smoke here.'"

"No, they say smoking is prohibited, for everyone."

"Ah, for everyone. For all those 'normal' people like you, right?" Andrzej screamed.

"Stop screaming, people are looking."

"What people? The normal people, like you?"

"Andrzej what's wrong with you?"

"Nothing, my love, absolutely nothing. Just that I have come to conclusion that through my own normalcy I forgot you are a woman, a female. You want for everything in your life to look normal. But that is not the case. I am not an average guy. I am Andrzej. I want to be a sexy guy who is next to a sexy woman. I smoke where I please and when I want to. Every day is a different experience and a separate event."

"Fine, you're right," Tina said, "Look, there is a waiter; he will ask you and you'll have to put down your cigar."

The waiter came up, looked at Andrzej and after a brief moment said "I will bring an ashtray. What would you like to drink?"

Andrzej recited the names of some drinks and dishes. Tina was quiet and his voice wasn't reaching her at all.

I want to be him so much, she thought, *yet everyday it seems that instead of getting closer to me, he drifts further away. I have no idea who he is, what does he want. He is like a jewel; miraculous, shining, magical yet...dead. Yes, dead.*

Andrzej grabbed her hand.

"Hey, Tina, are you here?"

"Yes, I'm sorry. I was just thinking hard."

"What would you like to drink? I ordered the food already."

"I'll have a martini."

"And a martini," the waiter repeated after her. He then turned around and marched towards the bar.

Andrzej was looking at her smiling.

"After this, I am taking you to an art gallery. Would you like to go?"

"Sounds great." Tina said.

The silence was then interrupted by the waiter.

"Here are the cocktails and it will be just a few minutes for your entrees."

"Thank you," Andrzej said.

"Oh you are very welcome. It is my pleasure serving you, sir."

"Serving you sir," Tina whispered, "what is that supposed to mean?"

"Oh nothing," Andrzej brushed off.

"What do you mean nothing? You are in a smoke-free restaurant puffing on your cigar. The waiter tells you he is getting a kick out of serving you, sir... Who are you, Andrzej?"

"This art exhibit I am taking you to is dedicated to..."

Tina stood from behind the table.

"I thought I loved you but I don't think that was love. Don't call me again. I wish you best of luck in everything that's important to you."

She left quickly while Andrzej was staring after her. The waiter came up:

"Ready for your dinner?"

"Ready," Andrzej replied.

"What about the plate for the lady?"

"Just put it down, go up to the bar and ask that woman over there if she would like to have dinner with me."

"No problem, sir."

After a while the waiter came back with a wide smile on his face.

"She accepted your invite," he announced.

"Great," Andrzej responded, "I hate eating alone."

He walked slowly down the street as the heels rhythmically resounded. He didn't like feeling clouded with thoughts and tried to push them away. He reached the gallery and walked in. He bought the ticket and moved towards the exhibit. He looked at one, the second painting but he couldn't focus. *What do women want from me?* The thoughts kept running through his head. He continued along the exhibit without paying much attention to the paintings. He saw a wicker bench and sat down. Now he was looking at the painting right across. It was very colorful, no shapes, just multitude of colors.

Interesting, he thought, *this is very much like life; colorful yet with no shape to it. When women try to shape me they lose the beauty of my freedom and harmony. Life is anxiety, a surprise that cannot be embodied in a shape. Once limited in a form, in a shape, life suffocates Life has to...live and not be suffocating. I like omen. I want them to be a part of my life but I cannot coexist with them. I like them near me and I hate when they want to be a part of me. It suffocates me. They have to serve me. Yes, they have to be for me, not with me. I want them all but only for a moment and this moment is worth eternity.*

As he kept on with those thoughts he scented perfume. He looked to see its source and saw her. Yes, it's the girl he fell in love with.

It's the chick from the cafe, he thought.

He got up and went to meet her; stood in front of her and gently grabbed her by the hand.

"Jordan?" he said it with a question in his voice.

First, she wanted to free her hand but allowed for it to remain in his instead.

"Yes," she responded.

"Do you remember? We met at the cafe?"

"Yes, I do remember very well."

"I didn't think I would see you again. I forgot to ask for your address, phone number or anything."

"Life surprises us in a nice way, sometimes" Jordan said with a smile.

"Yes, very much so."

"What are you doing at the gallery?" I didn't think you were an arts'' lover."

"I like music, arts and good book."

"And I like to dance," she said.

"Well, let's go and dance."

"Today?"

"Yes, today, now."

"Where?"

"Wherever there is music."

"Wait, I am not even dressed right."

"Clothes don't dance."

"I can see you really are up for some dancing."

"Yes, very much so, with you," Andrzej responded.

"Ok then, let's go but you pick the place."

They walked along the exhibit holding hands. Andrzej was back alive, happy and felt how life revives in him anew.

They danced for a long time; the slow and fast pieces alike. He held on to her hips, her arms, her breasts and she smothered his neck and gently his cheeks with her lips. They didn't talk. The music was doing all the talking. Andrzej bought of the DJ who kept playing what he asked for. The hall was swirling with lights as they themselves were in the midst of desire and understanding. Only on occasion they stared in each other's eyes. They wanted to read in them what was going to happen next and what the future holds. Did they get the answer? Probably not. Why to dream about tomorrow when now feels so great. They did not want to spoil this moment of happiness if that's what this was. They were together and perhaps that's what made it for the magical time when they felt connected with the invisible link they did not want to disentangle.

Love comes very unexpectedly. Love is dangerous. Love knows no boundaries and no obstacles. One doesn't have to know how to love. Love is what gives energy and willpower to create. Words are not necessary - the dictionary knows no appropriate terms which would give justice describing this incredible feeling. Love comes unexpectedly. It cannot be found. It comes on its own.

Music played uninterrupted as they swayed together on the floor, embraced with each other like some crazy couple who waited for wind to take kidnap them from this ocean of sensuality and drop in hands of reality.

* * *

Mark took off his golden Rolex and put in on the dresser. He went to the kitchen where a woman was going about the business.

"You know what I've noticed?" He asked.

"What is that?"

"Someone has been following me."

"No way."

"Yes. They've followed me in Chicago. They follow me here in Detroit."

"But who?"

"I don't know. First I thought it was something to do with the business but I was wrong."

"How can you be so sure?

"I know; trust me."

"Well maybe it is just a mistake. Maybe you're just imagining this."

"No, you know me. I wouldn't say something like this if I were not sure."

"I don't even know what it is that you do in the evenings. Sometimes you disappear for two days and I have no clue where you are. Maybe you do some shady things?"

"I help people. Don't worry about it."

"And I, your wife, cannot be helping them with you?"

"No, I don't think you would like it very much."

"How do you know?"

"I know, trust me."

"What if everything you say is just some excuses and there is some other woman in the picture?"

"What kind of nonsense is that?"

"One never knows – that's how it always starts. You disappear; at first for one day, then two and later for good."

"But you said you knew me and that nothing was able to surprise you."

"Yes, I know you and that's why I am afraid that you're cheating."

"Wow, wait a minute… Are you saying you were the one who hired those punks to follow me?"

"And what if it was me. So what?"

"That would change the whole situation."

"What situation?"

"The situation of our trust in each other."

"I am unable to trust you because you always lie."

"I don't lie to you. You are the one imagining some strange scenarios."

"Right. And the girl in Chicago is just a friend."

"Yes, a friend."

"Stop playing. Don't pretend and just tell the truth."

"I am telling the truth but I can see you are not interested in listening to the truth if it doesn't fit your script."

"This is not my script. It's your demeanor."

"Well, if that's how you think then let me define the truth to you the way I see it."

"Sure, if you want to!"

"In my opinion truth and lie do not exist. The truth today can be such and then become a lie tomorrow. I can lie today and then tomorrow it will turn out I said the truth. Truth and lie are things we create with eyes of imagination. We are under constant pressures; social, religious, political. We don't know what the truth is. We somehow feel entitled to make judgments about actions but we do not look into the causes. We accuse people that in our eyes they lie to us while if we only analyzed their acts it would turn out they were telling the truth.

Truth and lie are encoded in our brains and once we face reality we are scared to accept it. In order to defend our own concept of truth we are willing to perceive somebody as a liar while in reality he isn't one at all. Even if I spent a night with that girl in Chicago, to me that would be just an adventure while for you a betrayal. If you think you know me then what would be the reason for me to cheat on you? I don't want your answer right away but for you to think it all through. Love is not about following each other. Love is meant to be creative. If you love me let me be creative and don't drag me into the world of jealousy and suspicion. That way we would just create hell for each other."

"You are the one creating hell," the woman said.

"No, my dear. I live and I do what I think is right."

"I live too and I also do what I think is right," she answered angrily.

"In that case there is nothing left for us to say. If you don't like my lifestyle there is no point for us to be together."

"But it used to be so different some time ago," she continued.

"No, it has never been different. It's been the same all the time but you have started to think that you would be able to own me. I have never been and never will be yours."

"So why did you marry me?"

"I was hoping you needed me, that you would like to keep growing with your own pattern. I thought we both would need each other, in order to live."

"But I've done so much for you and helped you with so many things."

"Yes, but out of what intentions?"

"Because I love you."

"You think that you love me but that's not love. You thought you were investing in me. You wanted to own me, like a dog or a parrot. You became scared and that's where you got lost. Fear paralyzed your thoughts. You no longer were a woman but became a wife. You no longer care about my life. Now you look at that piece of paper called Marriage Certificate and think that legally I am yours. You probably are right here but so what? I am further away from you than I have ever been before. I am drifting away from you to infinity, where my place is. You will feel awful. You may even hate me to the point where you wish me death but in fact those would be just your impressions. Those feelings of hate and anger no longer reach me though, because in my life they no longer mean anything. I am free, free from the truth and lie, free from relationship which only limited my right to be myself. I have no opinion about you. I can't say I don't like you or that I have no respect for you. I have to leave for my world, the one that was created for me. Apparently our marriage was not meant to last forever. Treat this as an adventure and be yourself without me. Maybe you will be better off this way. You won't have to worry where I am and what I do. Now you are free so do what suits you best so that your life is more fulfilling. If you don't grow then it will ultimately mean that for your entire life you have been nothing but a jealous materialist whose goal in life was collecting of more and more: house, car, dog, cat, husband and so on... Be yourself and when you see that it is hard then you think, think deep who you really are. You are the only one who knows the truth and this is the only and ultimate truth, the one that you cannot interpret. No environment or knowledge can influence it. This is you. Yes, the truth is you with yourself. You cannot lie yourself. It's impossible. You cannot talk yourself into something that isn't authentic.

"Stop it!" the woman yelled, "Stop with this nonsense! You must think you're some kind of philosopher with answers to everything. You think you can just solve everything while in fact you're noting but a liar. You lie and this has become your life. I don't love you anymore because you've lied to me. I want nothing to do with you. You've wasted four years of my life. I did everything you asked for. I thought you were happy with me, that you loved me, that you would be mine and mine alone!"

She had burst into tears.

"Mine and mine alone..." Mark repeated quietly.

He came up to the woman and wanted to hold her but she pushed him away.

"Get the hell out of this house!" She yelled after a moment.

"Ok," Mark responded, "but at the end I want to add that it was you who followed me and not the other way around."

He went into the room, put his Rolex on and quickly directed himself towards the door. He opened it and looked at the woman.

"Get the fuck out! She screamed.

He turned the head away and shut the door behind him. He got into his car, started off the engine as the black BMW murmured *by success for it will itself change into a failure. Likewise one cannot only be experiencing failures - that would mean I am plain stupid. What is my life?*

He drove with average speed looking at times at cars passing by, stared at the horizon and the sky set with thousands of stars. When we are by ourselves, with no witnesses to watch us, nature becomes our best friend. It can be the starry night, murmuring trees, peaceful stream or angry ocean. Whatever this would be – nature listens to us. We become a part of it and we can always count on it.

At least that was Mark's impression. He stared at that starry night and felt free and relaxed.

What are my successes and my failures in comparison to this sky? He thought. Is it worth worrying that something didn't turn out the way I wished? Up there everything is happening according to some organized chaos while here, on earth we must have everything organized to perfection. From the very beginning of the world we could never appreciate it. We drive ourselves towards disaster. We think we are the smartest. We created everything against us. Law, politics, religion – it is all nonsense. Why don't we look at the nature and learn from its example? Why do we have to change everything to the point where we act against common sense and logic? We make promises only to break them. We betray friends, rape children, beat up old people, attack the defenseless, live in relationships for money, and teach to hate and to lie... We change history and artificially substitute love with sex. The natural beauty we turn into pornography. We turn a woman into wife and a man into husband. I am here, by myself now – Mark kept thinking – so what if I don't like any of it? I do what I can to show the world that there are things which ought not to be betrayed. There are values which should never be questioned and history that cannot be changed for it is authentic. Is anyone listening? I don't know but up there, somewhere in the space there is the law that runs the natural course of cosmos. The perpetual motion; I know there is no beginning and no end. This is what keeps me in the constant motion and gives energy. I want to create not fight against the purposeless actions of another human beings who lost their values. Will I have enough strength? I don't know and I am not worried about it because one day I may run into someone who thinks the same way I do, and then they may have friends who are on the same page as well. Then the theory will have its proof that

In the universe everything takes place in a pre-programmed mode. This is when what I said would be proven: love is the only natural sensation given to us from the very beginning. We can't find it but once we do, the civilization will take the new course. Common sense and love will create the new world, free from politics, religion and this is when we will have paradise on earth. We haven't discovered that paradise yet because we haven't grown to it. Only few can identify with nature and enjoy life. Let's listen to them. It doesn't cost us anything. Let's listen to the voice of our heart and not the reason which is corrupt. Let's listen to the heart. I would so want to love but I have to wait yet – love needs to be waited to. It will come on its own with no protest.

BMW kept on moving down the freeway. Mark drove thinking deeply. The neons with advertisements and various signs flashed on and on with temptation. Mark paid them no attention though. He drove, which he liked to do very much as it felt calming to be the driver. To be a driver meant to be responsible for others. The driver holds his life in his hands. He also holds in his hands the lives of others. To be a good driver is not just to be able to pass by others. A good driver can foresee things and doesn't look for others to put the blame on. A good driver makes decisions quickly. He doesn't fear death. A good driver is full of respect for death. A good driver is sober and ready to bring help to others when needed. A good driver loves people. Mark is a good driver.

He exited the freeway and entered Telegraph Rd. heading towards his favorite hotel. He no longer had a house or wife. He only had himself. He didn't like solitude but he did enjoy freedom.

Tomorrow is going to be a very interesting day, he thought. *Yes, definitely. Tomorrow is going to be interesting...*

* * *

It is September, 2007. The United states are in the process of conducting the meaningless occupation of Iraq. The President and his entire clique continue trying to sell their political cheap slogans thinking this will gain the sympathy of the people. On top of it by now there are loud conversations about the possibility of war with Iran. Greed and hunger for power have no boundaries. Corruption, theft, and lie – that is all that the tactics of politicians-thugs has achieved. Could this be the beginning off the end of the United States? That is a possibility. One cannot run politics based on weapons and soldiers. Inflation and the corrupt banking system rooted in putting interest rates on money that has no value leads to ruin of budgets and not just the American ones but worldwide. Religions begin to take on political forms. More and more religious politicians come out with the conviction that all people in the world should believe in God represented by liars. The educational system in the world is collapsing. Children lose ambitions while the youth are scared of making decisions. Nobody is taking risks as it makes no sense to risk anything. Our lives are now limited to collection of goods which we do not even need. We talk about money, religion and politics. Business has kicked out all other areas of our lives. There is no common sense. There are ridiculous laws though and strictly business oriented perspective on the world. Marriage for money. A child for money. Love for money. Friendship for money. We have lived on this planet for thousands of years and that is all we can afford. It's sad but true. Good people do not play politics and they do not play religion. Good people are aware of what's going on but they are helpless. There is no way to fight those whose only purpose is power and money. The have never been loved and so they will never be able to create things out of love. They will be destroying everything they encounter on their routes. They are dead while alive. They are not human beings but robots. The 21st Century hasn't brought us anything new. We have a chance though to grow to prosperity. Let's be honest with our neighbors. Let's tell each other we love each other. It doesn't hurt. Let's try to do something for others without looking for what's in it for us. Let's love ourselves. Let's not identify the word "love" with a sexual act. Love is a way of life and not a one-time adventure. We can live better. There are many politicians -patriots but they have been pushed to the side. Let's get them out from the shadows and help, so they can work for us and for our good.

Maybe one day there will come about the modern humanity, the humanity whose goal will be to rejoice and dance, in other words: to live. Planet Earth will no longer be divided into countries. The borders will disappear as well as all religions. We will no longer teach love. Let's give love a chance to be a natural factor. There will be a Council of Civilization of which focus will be to prevent conflicts, division of technologies and spread of prosperity. We will get rid of nuclear power. There will be no political parties and every citizen will have his number confirmed with his finger print. The citizens of the world will vote directly the candidates for the Council of Civilization. Everyone will have the right to define themselves, meaning being able to have some basic expectations from life. If you want to be a farmer – you'll be a farmer. If you want to be a businessman – you will be one. When the world budget is defined there will be no percentages or interest rates on money. The money will have the actual value in goods. This will take care of inflation since the currency will now have some real value. People will be able to retire at the age of 40 or 50 and will have the time to teach the kids and the youth. They will have time for travel and play. The billion dollar debts will disappear. There will be some who are wealthier but there will be no poor people. We will satisfy the needs of the entire civilization. Political aspirations will be gone as will the armies. There will be no more races for power because authority will be rooted in quest for support and development of the civilization. Land will not have a price because it belongs to itself. There will be cap on wealth which will be satisfactory to those more operative and better educated individuals. In fact we do not need much in order to enjoy life. There will be no inheritance and no power of money. Let's allow each citizen to live right from the beginning. Let's stop showering the kids with million dollar fortunes but let them live their lives through. Let's not take away their opportunity to make mistakes. Let's allow everyone to live.

Once we start putting our energies and knowledge for good causes we will eliminate hunger, the global warming; we'll clean up the atmosphere and will be able to live on earth the way we were meant to live. The judicial system will be simplified because crimes committed as the result of lacking the means to live will be eliminated. When we love naturally and when we are financially secure there will be no more drug deals and no more weapons trades.

Weapons will disappear from the face of the earth and will be only used by the Council of Civilization sporadically with the purpose of protection of the values of the "New World." When we stop worrying about the future we will learn to live today. This will be the highest stadium of our civilization on Earth.

* * *

"Mr. Andrzej!" an older man yelled upon coming to the office.

"What happened?" Andrzej asked.

"That insurance company that we talked about yesterday, they refused to pay up."

"Bastards," Andrzej said.

"That's not all," the man continued.

"What is it?"

"The accuse us that that building that burnt down was set on fire deliberately to collect the insurance money."

"That building was bought to serve the single mothers organization. What good would it do to burn down something that had served such noble cause? They have nowhere to go. Even if the insurance paid up the women still would be unable to live off of that amount."

"Yes, yes," the man kept repeating. "There is one trick to it though."

"What?" Andrzej asked surprised.

"Well, it turns out this building belonged to those women."

"What does it mean 'belonged'?" Andrzej asked.

"That means somebody bought this building two months ago without letting us know."

"Damn it!" Andrzej yelled. "That's impossible!"

"And yet…"

"Who bought the building?"

"I am not sure yet but I will know tomorrow."

"Incredible," Andrzej said. "No matter where you move there is dirt and garbage everywhere."

"No need to be angry," the man tried to say.

"What are you talking about?" Andrzej continued. "I thought I did something good and here it turns out that just took advantage of me. I placed those women. They are clueless about anything."

"That doesn't matter. They love you."

"I know but besides that they also have to live somewhere and have to have a place to raise the kids."

"Please do not get upset so much. We'll see, something will work out."

"Don't be so sure. Somebody bought this building and wants to make money off of it. There is nothing wrong with that but the intentions are different. Whoever it was cheated me and the women."

"So what can you do now?"

"Right now nothing."

Andrzej got up off of the chair and started to pace.

They gave me a job, he thought, *and I thought I would help them make a few dollars. All that was false. They have used me too.*

He walked up to the telephone and dialed a number.

"Hello," he heard on the other end.

"Hi John," he answered.

"Oh, cool that you're calling. I was thinking about buzzing you," John said.

"Oh yeah? About what?"

"About that house for single mothers."

"Oh yeah! What? Are you thinking about construction work around that building?" Andrzej said ironically.

"No, no, that building went down in flames. The insurance will pay around 750 thousands and thus we will have the cash for down-payment for that high rise in Chicago."

"It all sounds good but what is going to happen with those women?"

"That isn't our problem."

"How come?"

"It's not and that's it. What is it?"

"Well it is that I had promised those women a better future."

"Oh, Andrzej have some common sense. You cannot promise people something that is merely a utopian stack of dreams."

"But you've promised me," Andrzej started.

"Hey, Andrzej, come on. I promised but in the business language."

"What do you mean by 'business language'?"

"The business language, my man, is the language where all words have two different meanings."

"Bull crap," Andrzej said.

"No, it isn't bull crap. For instance the word 'promised' in normal language means you guarantee. In the business language it means 'don't count on me'."

"Keep going, go ahead," Andrzej kept saying. "What else can you tell me?"

"Take a look at the word 'impossible'. Normally it would mean something that is not possible. In the business language it means something will cost more. The next example is the word 'partnership'. Normally it brings to mind cooperation an understanding. In the business language is means rivalry. Do you want more examples?"

"No, that's enough," Andrzej answered. "It looks like we live in some very abstract dimensions of vocabulary."

"That's it!" John exclaimed.

"Ok, I should have known this and maybe I even have but just for a split second I wanted to be a human being."

"Hey, Andrzej, don't melt. Life goes on. Go ahead, find some girl and enjoy life."

"Easy to say. Maybe the girls have their own vocabulary too with words that sound the same but mean something different."

John was quiet.

"Are you there?" Andrzej asked.

"Yes, I am but I have to run. I don't have time to waste on talking with you about some junk. Once we get the money I will let you know."

"Ok, let know. Oh, well tell me finally who set it on fire?"

"The East side gang guys," John responded.

"Ok, talk to you later," Andrzej finished.

He put the phone down and sat in the chair.

Who am I? Who I would like to be? I have to change something in my life. No matter what I touch it always ends in some scam. I know this is a scam but when I look around I see that scam is generally accepted. Everybody cheats and lies. The insurance companies, the radio advertisements, politicians and priests alike. There is no concept of truth and lie anymore. There is just the broad interpretation of expressions.

He got up from the seat and approached the telephone again. Gently he dialed the number.

"Hello," the voice on the other end said.

"Good morning," Andrzej responded.

"Oh, Mr. Andrzej," smiley voice answered. "It's so nice to hear your voice."

"Oh yes?" Andrzej answered irritated.

"Of course it is always good to see you or hear your voice at least."

"Ms. Virginia, I'm calling because I have found out what had happened. I am very sorry."

"Don't worry. Somehow we will manage."

"No, you will not. What are you going to do now?"

"We are looking for some place where we can stay temporarily."

"Who is going to take thirty women with children?"

"It is not easy but we hope that somehow, one by one, we will find a locum, even if separately."

"But in a group things were so much easier for you and so much safer. You were able to take turns who takes care of the children..."

"Yes, it is true. You have organized it all so nicely and everything worked just perfectly. Now we have to start from scratch."

"I do have an idea," Andrzej said.

"What idea is this, Mr. Andrzej?"

"Well, I have decided to help you once more. This time I will buy the building and I will do it myself alone. I have some savings. What do I need that money for anyway? So, I will buy you a building where you will live like before. You will be paying me rent, whatever you can afford, and the rest I will cover. I will cover the cost of fixings if there is a need to. Each of the young mothers will have a chance to get some education. I am not necessarily saying colleges or something. You will learn some crafts, like some basic machine operating, computer accounting, nurse aide, kindergarten teacher, barmaids, waitresses, etc. We will have a theater and musical groups. For the money you earn you will be able to go to theaters and orchestra hall. You will live. I don't want you to be prostitutes or drug addicts. With time, each one of you will gain a sense of confidence and will be able to support yourself. The kids, once they grow up, will be able to provide for themselves too. Mothers do not have to help the kids throughout their entire life. It only takes away the kids' ability to make decisions. You have to believe in yourself and you will, no doubt, succeed."

"What you're saying sounds so brilliant. The girls, once they hear it, will certainly be happy to have this chance."

"I hope they all accept my idea. Tomorrow I will find the building where within a month you would be able to move in. For now only try to make it at the shelters. There should be some space."

"Thank you very much, from the bottom of my heart Virginia. I will keep in touch with you and make sure that the girls are fine, with no drinking and no drugs."

"Thanks, Virginia," Andrzej finished and put down the phone.

At the same moment the telephone rang. Andrzej picked up. It was Jordan.

"Hi babe," she greeted him.

Andrzej's heartbeat picked up and he felt goose bumps all over his arms. He liked her voice and it filled him up with peace and sentiment.

"What's going on?" He asked.

"Nothing new but I wanted to see you."

"That's great," Andrzej was genuinely happy. "Champagne and candles?"

"Sounds good," she replied.

"Seven p.m. At my house," Andrzej said.

"Seven p.m. Then," Jordan confirmed.

Andrzej put the phone down and jumped he was so happy.

"She likes me. Who knows? She may even love me!" He yelled.

He put the suit jacket on and ran out to the parking lot. He got in his car and took off quickly to the cafe.

Roses and candles, he thought, *what a great combination.*

He kept driving fast down the road, pulled up by the flower shop, got inside and screamed at the door: "Twenty one yellow lemon roses and five red candles."

"You've got it, sir Andrzej," the woman answered right away.

She knew him as he was used to buying flowers there which was not a habit of an average American. They do not buy flowers just out of the blue and for no reason. They give flowers "for something" while he was doing it purely for his satisfaction. Women liked flowers and he enjoyed giving those to them. The bouquet looked fantastic and the roses smelled great. Andrzej got in the car and started off again with the tires squeaking. It was time for the wine shop.

Little sparks of candles vividly danced in their own lively motion. The bottle of wine and flowers harmoniously filled up the room atmosphere.

Andrzej was sitting at the table looking at Jordan. She looked mysterious surrounded by flowers and in the flash of the candles. He liked this scenario. He wasn't talking much for that reason – he didn't want to ruin the magical mood. She softly touched the edge of the wine glass with her lips, not saying much. Just listening to music and feeling the wine warming up her cheeks.

"You look so beautiful," he finally broke the silence.

"Thank you."

"No, don't thank me – it's a fact."

"Even if it is, it's good to say thank you for noticing."

"You're right, I guess. But what is it that you wanted to chat about?"

Jordan moved in her chair somewhat uncomfortable. She looked embarrassed. She was staring at Andrzej's eyes in search for any help. His eyes were both hot and cold at the same time; not the eyes of someone beaming with warmth onto others. One could say his eyes were summoning things up or evaluating. One could easily fall in love with them but this would be one unhappy love for those eyes were dictating and filled with indescribable power. Jordan was scared to start but finally broke the ice.

"Well," she began calm, "I asked you to meet me because I have something important to tell you."

"Go ahead, I'm listening."

"Well, our situation, meaning you and I," she was talking somewhat disorderly and she realized this but could not control herself.

"Take your time," Andrzej tried to calm her down. "You don't have to be nervous. You're not in court."

"I know," she quietly said, "but what I want to say is not easy for me."

Andrzej seemed surprised.

"What is it you want to tell me?"

"Ok, I like you very much, Andrzej, and I know that you are intelligent, handsome, have great manners and are very sensitive."

"This time I thank you," Andrzej said with a smile.

"Nothing to thank me for," she continued. "You said it yourself that I am attractive, energetic…"

"Yes," Andrzej interrupted.

"But my circumstances aren't all that good as it may seem. I am in a lot of debt and have no money to pay the rent. On the other side my car is old by now, starts to act out and soon I am going to have to get a new one. My father has lost his job and now I have to be helping him now. I would like to go to Italy to meet artists and models. I would also like a bigger office and I need more space to conduct business."

"Slow down, slow down," Andrzej interrupted again. "Why are you telling me all this?"

Jordan looked at him with no particular expression.

"I am telling you this so you can understand that I cannot see you anymore."

Andrzej looked at her in disbelief.

"What are you talking about?" He asked.

"Exactly what you hear," she quietly replied.

"Have I offended you somehow?"

"No."

"So what is this whole story of your problems about?"

"I need money," she answered.

"I am not a bank," Andrzej said angrily.

"I know you're not," Jordan continued, "but you could help me."

"Help you lose my money? How do you imagine that?"

"You could buy me a car and pay for my apartment."

"Hey, hey, has it occurred to you that you have been running your business for five years now and since you are short on money to live off, then there might be something wrong with the business?"

"You're wrong. My business is fine and it's just the matter of money to give it some kick."

"Give it some kick?" Andrzej asked upset now. "How can you give a kick to a business that hasn't been paying off?"

Silence filled the room and Jordan looked straight ahead not saying anything.

"Hey!" Andrzej yelled. "I am talking to you! How can you give a kick to business that has not paid off?"

"You don't want to help me. You don't understand me," she said.

"And I think that it is you who doesn't understand me," Andrzej replied. "If after five years of running a business you have no money it means that either it is crappy business or you don't know how to run it."

"Don't offend me like that!" Jordan exclaimed.

"I am not trying to offend you. I am simply telling you things you don't want to hear."

"That's not true. I am listening to you."

"If you do, then believe me and take a look at your situation."

"The bottom line is that you don't want to help me," she said crying.

"I want to save you, kiddo. It is not the matter of help but the matter of your views and principles."

"You don't want to help me," she just kept on repeating. "You don't want to do anything for me. I thought you cared about me."

Andrzej got up from behind the table, came up to Jordan and reached for her hand. He passed her the jacket and helped to put it on. He grabbed her hand and took outside, opened his car and helped her to it. Turning back on the heel he walked back to the house. He sat at the table and poured a glass of wine.

I love her, he thought. *And so what? This is love for me alone. She doesn't love me and probably never would. I found my love and was proud of it. I thought I knew how to love but I was wrong. I've got my love and so what? There is just the feeling that's left and all the rest just disappeared in the air. Maybe this was not love? What is this love then? Damn it!*

* * *

Senator Hendrix was sitting in his office with computer in front of him. His forehead covered with sweat and hands shaking but he just kept on writing with determination. The letter was entitled "To the Citizens Who Trusted Me." It was meant to be emailed to the New York Times.

It read:

Dear Fellow Citizens;

I apologize right at the beginning that I personally cannot tell you this but the course of events and their consequences are so unpleasant I am unable to look in anyone's eyes right now.

From the very first day when I was elected by you to represent you, I have done absolutely nothing to fulfill any of my campaign promises. It was not as the result of my ignorance. I have always wanted to be a god citizen, respect the Constitution and be loved by thousands of my constituents. The reality turned out to be much worse than I expected. I have come to conclusion that politics has nothing to do with representing anyone. It lives according to its own life, totally disconnected from the interests of the society. Politicians do not solve problems. They create them. I have always wanted that the education of our children be the top priority for us. I wanted to create the educational system which would, indeed, shape up well the future, bright citizens. During my term I was forced, however, to cut funds for education and to cut teachers' pay. I also wanted for all people to be able to have access to health care. In reality though, I voted for legislation that was against the common health care access. I wanted for our retirees to have good and dignified twilight of life, so they can enjoy their senior years. In reality I supported the law which took away chances for all that from them. I hate war and the thought of it gives me goose bumps. When President Bush was initiating the war in Iraq I was the first one to support the vote for "yes" for this war. I don't like homosexual deviations but I voted for the right of homosexuals to get married. I wanted to help the hungry but I vote against sending money to Africa.

You may ask me why did I do all of that? I would have to answer that I was given offers I could not turn down. These companies which were giving me millions of dollars for the campaign, paid for my vacation, gave bribes – they all expected results. After the tragedy of the New Orleans the insurance companies did not give money to those who suffered but to the giant corporation that scammed people when they needed help. The pharmaceutical companies, banks, environmentalists, education and so called culture; they are all property of big corporations. I am sorry to tell you this but this is the reality.

Today I decided to tell you the truth. I cannot live with this any longer. I lied to you and I lied myself. I can no longer live like this. I am asking for your forgiveness!"

Henrix finished writing, took a breath and moved away from the computer.

"Sounds alright?" He asked the man sitting across from him.

"Yes, we don't have much time," the stranger said.

"I understand," Henrix nodded, "but you do have the list of all those corporations that were paying me off."

"Yes, I do and I would like to thank you for that, Senator."

"Please do not call me 'Senator'. I don't deserve this."

"Why not?"

"I have betrayed my constituents, my country and myself. I am nobody."

"Yes, but were doing it all under pressure."

"There is no such excuse ass 'under pressure'. I have made the decisions and I have to face their consequences."

"I feel bad for you, Mr. Henrix," the stranger said.

"Please, do not get sentimental here. You are the one who came here with this stack of papers. You are the one who proved I have been a corrupt bandit. You are the one with proofs in your hand. Now you're telling me you feel sorry for me?"

"Yes. I am not lying to you. I do feel sorry. What I did was not aimed against you."

"I know, I know that. How do you plan to take it with those large corporations though?"

"I don't have a plan yet but talking to you is a good start."

"I hope what I wrote today along with all the materials I gave you will help in continuation of this noble idea."

"Thank you," the stranger said.

"I have one more request for you," Henrix added.

"Go ahead, I am listening."

"Once this whole ordeal is over, please tell my son that I was a patriot."

"You have my word."

"Well," Henrix said, "that would be it. Do you have the gun?"

"Yes, here you are," the man said giving Senator Henrix the gun.

Henrix grabbed it.

"You have a nice watch," he said.

"Thank you," the stranger replied.

"Is it Rolex?"

"Yes."

"Golden?"

"Yes." Senator put the gun in his mouth and pulled the trigger. Bang!!!

The stranger got off the seat and looked at the senator's body. Without a hurry he came up to the computer and clicked 'send' button. He left the office and in a calm manner walked down the hallway. He came out to the parking lot and got in his car. Starting slowly he joined the street traffic. After a few minutes he stopped; with a skilled motion he grabbed his face and shook it. Fake cheeks and fake mustache fell off. The man got out of his car and continued down the street on foot. On the way he threw the mask into a garbage can. He walked calm. He was satisfied.

Time for rest, he thought.

On the corner he got into another car; started off the engine and took off. He reached the airport in thirty minutes; returned the car at the rental and soon was comfortable in a seat on the airplane. Pleasant flight attendant asked if he needed a drink. He ordered champagne.

Ah, what the hell, he thought. *I had a good day.*

He arrived in Detroit somewhat late; found his car on the parking lot and drove onto the freeway. After forty minutes or so he pulled up by some club.

Ah, he thought; *I might as well stop by for a drink. It is not that late yet. The it's not like I have to be in a hurry to be somewhere anymore. For a moment I forgot I no longer had a wife.* He stood at the club's entrance. The golden sign said: "Excalibur" shining on the frontal wall. A young guy who parked cars appeared so fast by his car door that Mark was nearly shocked.

"How did you get here?" Mark asked.

"I'm quick, huh?" The young fellow replied.

"Yes, very much so," Mark confirmed.

"You do not come here too often."

"No, not really."

"Maybe something will change tonight?" The youngster said almost with hope.

"Who know? Who knows?"

"Have a good time."

"Thanks a lot."

Mark walked into the club and once his eyes got used to the lights he spotted a girl who was sitting at the desk. Her short hair was rounding a beautiful face. He noticed her green eyes; walked up to the desk.

"Good evening," he said.

"Welcome to 'Excalibur'," the girl responded.

Mark felt his shoulders tense. Her voice was warm, so warm he wanted to grab and hold her in his arms to absorb some of that warmth.

"What's your name?" He asked her.

"Kate."

"But you speak with an accent. Where are you from?"

"From Poland."

"So nice to see an angel from across the ocean," Mark joyfully said.

"Oh, so you speak Polish as well?"

"Of course. I was born there."

"Not too many Poles come here," she told him. "Majority of patrons are well-off Americans and Italians. Arabs are mighty too. They hold their mafia meetings."

"You are very well orientated about your clientele," Mark said.

"I have to. It's my job. They pay me for it.
"Well, what exactly do you do here?"

"I take reservations, order drinks, wine, whiskey; I purchase cigars and order girls for companion. Besides that I organize some fashion shows and wine tasting evenings."

"That's a lot of things to do," Mark noticed. "Do they pay you well?"

"I don't complain but I am getting tired of it. They all would love to just sleep with me."

"Don't hold it against them. It's instinct."

"Well, you can control instincts," Kate responded.

"That's true, Katie. Can I call you that?"

"Sure. I don't mind. What is your name?"

"Mark."

"Can I call you Mr. Mark then?"

"Just Mark."

"That's not appropriate."

"Let's not talk about what's appropriate and what isn't for a moment. I want you to call me Mark."

"Fine, if you, Mr. … oops, if you, Mark, insist. What table do you want?"

"What do you have available?"

"VIP, the regular tables, ones closer to the host and tall bar seats."

"I would like a table surrounded by the magical circle of your dreams, the one where the most secret thoughts can materialize. I want a table with no sense of the past or the present, where future is the unknown abbeys of hope; where there is no need to say yes or no and where everything happens with the natural cycle of life instinct – a table of love, please."

Kasia listened to Mark passionately. She like listening to him and it just made her feel good. For the first time she felt like herself. He was something she has been waiting for. He talked and she just wanted to listen.

"Say something more," she whispered.

"I can talk infinitely and I know you will keep listening. I am sure of that. For the first time in my life I am sure of something. Everything I have done so far was based on rules; law, justice, friendship and love. But I was clueless when it comes to love. It comes suddenly, like death. Earlier today I saw death and now I have met love. Comparing the two I really do not see the difference. Death symbolizes victory while love brings to my mind liberation. I want to be free and I thought I was. Now I know I was wrong. From the moment I saw you I no longer am who I was. I am proud now of whom I am now. I am telling you all this because I know you want to know all of it, to make sure that what you feel is real."

He reached gently for her hand. She didn't resist. He saw her eyes and she was crying. From far away somewhere the sounds of music were coming rhythmically. The guests leaving the establishment didn't even try to invade into their moment. Some nodded while others ignored them but with a smile.

The war in Iraq continues. Hungry people keep dying. New York is full of life of both the poor and the rich. In Warsaw somebody is reading a poem while in the parliament the politicians keep arguing over silly things. Babies are born and teenagers die. The climate keeps warming up. Putin is giving high fives because the price of gas keeps rising. Nobody even noticed that in Detroit love has been born in just one split of a second. It didn't need the nuclear power or negotiations of some politicians. It needed no rabbi and no priest. The love was born out of its own.

At the same time a silver Corvette parked in front of the club.

"Ah! Mr. Andrzej!" The boy yelled running up to the car. Andrzej put a twenty dollar bill in his hand. He wanted to say something.

"No need to say anything," the youngster spoke ahead of him. "It will be parked in the same spot as usual."

Andrzej smiled and walked energetically towards the entrance. As he came in the very first thing he noticed in the hallway was them... He stood puzzled. He came up closer. He was looking at Kasia and the well-dressed man holding her hand. He wanted to say something but stopped himself. He enjoyed the situation and felt like he was a part of it. Kasia spoke first:

"Oh, hi Andrzej. Welcome. You want your table?"

"Maybe you could introduce me first to your new admirer."

"Yes, excuse me. This is Mark."

The men exchanged handshakes. Andrzej wanted to test the other one and he squeezed his hand as strong as possible. He was surprised to notice that hand didn't go soft at all. Quite the opposite, the handshake was firm and unmoved.

"You are from Poland as well?" Andrzej asked.

"Yes, I have come thirty years ago."

"Not bad. I have been in the United States for twenty years now. Would you like to join my table? Andrzej offered.

Kasia was looking at Andrzej with uncertainty. There was a time she considered him her boyfriend and was scared he would start making some stupid remarks but not at all. That didn't happen.

"Do you mind if I join Andrzej?" Mark asked.

"Not at all, of course," Kasia answered relieved. She needed a moment of solitude to sum up everything that happened in such short period of time.

The two men walked towards the table.

* * *

Death of Senator Henrix caused an uproar in political circles. The telephones were off the hook and emails were circling the country. An hour after his suicide all TV networks ran the scandalous documentation on corruption and lawlessness in the business world. Panic spread around. Events took the domino effect course. Reporters were embarrassed as well as some of the information pertained to corruption in the media world. There was no time to interpret things. All large corporations like FOX, NBC, and ABC were disseminating facts which now took the turn against them. Chaos paralyzed the censorship. The President and his cabinet were totally discredited. Senators and the big-shots of the business world turned out to be bandits and thieves. Some of the facts pointed out the murderers and flat out thugs. The Pandora's Box got wide open. Information about releasing names of American agents by the American government also got out. Tortures of prisoners, phone bugs, Geneva Convention abuse – all this was happening in the country portrayed as an example of Democracy. Contracts with China for billions of dollars on merchandise items sent later to America that are flat out junk with addition of poison; enhanced tooth paste, kiddy toys with lead based paint, car tires completely out of compliance with any standards. The great America now taking shit for gold. The Chinese government got gazillions of dollars in government warranties. The American ports are now in Arab hands. For all this we fund the Olympics in China. China has already America in its hands. Arabs are looking for ways to get even for U.S. Support of Israel. What's left is Cuba. One cannot do business with Cuba and cannot smoke their cigars. After the entire Cuban product could "overtake" the American market and ruin the American economy. Cuba needs to be kept short on the leash. One thing gets missed in it though and it's the fact that it was Cub which first offered Americans help after hurricane Katrina hit, the one that completely evened out New Orleans to the ground. Of course the proud American government declined any support from the communist Cuba. Instead, the Chinese language schools are booming.

Death of Senator Henrix shook up all the interested. It is just the illusionary beginning of the end. In this pile of garbage we have reached already the point when we ourselves no longer know what is reality and what is fiction. Is Senator Henrix someone factual or just a product of one's imagination? Is common sense something real or just a fiction? If it is real then what is common sense? Is corruption a result of common sense? If so why should we oppose politicians and business people? There is only one answer to this. We know for sure what good and evil is. If we are certain that something is evil, then it is. That's all there is to it. Let's not try to excuse and explain anything. Evil is just that – evil, and will remain such always. There is no alternative.

Let's be ourselves. Let's stop listening to others and let's stand on the side of good. Let's respect and cherish it!

***

Mark began the conversation in an unexpected way. Andrzej was looking at him and listened.

"The candidates for the U.S. Presidency," Mark started; "try to portray themselves in the best light possible to the public. They don't believe in God, yet they claim they do. They don't care about the kids but they claim they will provide for them. They don't care about the elders but they claim they will look after their interests. In reality they don't care about anything besides their own careers. They want to have the satisfaction that comes with leadership, giving orders of life-death value. They want to prove to others, liars like themselves, that they are better. There is no point believing in those people because a properly thinking human being with average intelligence and ability to put things together will never believe in this multitude of lies. Election itself appears to be lacking something. Nobody knows who can and who cannot vote or weather somebody is controlling the election. Why the one most liked by the citizens never wins? Why there is always some other option in situations where common sense dictates there is none? Why do we live in fear of things we should never fear? Why do we learn fake love and not how to control hate? There is no good and let's face it: all the evil things in this world we have created ourselves. The statement: "That's what was meant to happen" is stupid. We are the only ones who are guilty here in how we allow the ignorant and greedy crazies run our lives. Ron Paul is the only candidate for the U.S presidency who is the true human being to the core. Is he going to win? No, and he himself doesn't believe he will since, as he had pointed out, he would not be able to raise a hundred million dollars. Who will win then? The one who will have the hundred million dollars. Is anything going to change? No. I have been always an optimist but I do not think that anything will change in this world ran by rules of the unnaturally created system. This is all we can afford. We cannot afford anything else; sad but true.

The third world war is inevitable. We are unable to satisfy the political ambitions of people who never have loved anything and anyone. The only thing that matters is their political aspirations. It could have been so much different. It should be so much different. This mess cannot last forever. I am powerless but I have love. My love is untouched by impure desire. It is natural. I love the entire world and all the people. I love life. Do not count, however, that if someone somewhere someday slaps me, that I will, out of love, present the second cheek. Out of love I will fire up the fatal punch in the nose of the enemy who thinks he taught me how to love.

All in all there are more reasonable people around than the crazies. Good and love usually wins. Let's not surrender and fall under oppression and if the heart says "do not vote", then don't. If there is no candidate whom you feel you can trust – don't vote. They will, after all, do to you whatever they will feel like doing.

We have bastardized already all constitutions and laws. The worst is, however, that we have lost the right to common sense. It is hard to live like this but hope is stronger than lies.

Someday the Sun will rise like at the beginning of the creation. I will open my eyes and see that it happened! My dreams came true."

"Why are you saying all this? Andrzej asked.

"Because I needed to vent," Mark answered.

"I have to tell you that I am surprised. We have only known each other for a few minutes and you get deeply into subjects of politics and worlds affairs."

"Whom can I talk to honestly if not with another Pole abroad?" Mark asked with a smile.

"Ha ha!" Andrzej laughed. "You're right. Well, let me tell you something now, OK?"

"Shoot," Mark answered.

"It will not be about politics or money," Andrzej began.

"Thanks God," Mark said enthusiastically.

"Well, I will honestly tell you that throughout my entire life I have been looking for love and once I am very close to finding it, it just slips away. I have never really paid attention to it but recently I have looked at my feelings from a different angle. I sum up the events and come to conclusion that there is no point to look for love. As the matter of fact I will tell you that I have loved many women in my life, really. I don't know why I have never stayed with one. Could be that there is something wrong with me? Maybe I don't know how to love? I would like to stay with one woman and love, love indefinitely. It seems so simple but not for me. This constant chase after women tires me but once I have one, after some time I am ready to just quit everything and be alone until the moment comes when the next one appears on the horizon. What is it?"

Mark was looking at him with great deal of attention. He wasn't saying anything, just gathered together things and after a while said:" Are you happy with your life?"

"Yes. I will tell you in all honesty that I am. I have been through a lot of good and bad stuff but I have never had regrets about my decisions. In general yes, I am happy."

"Have women ever been an obstacle to your plans?"

"Yes, always. They intrude when our relationships seem to be stable and lasting."

"So for what sake do you lead to situations when relationships are lasting?"

"I don't know. I don't like being alone."

"That is not a reason to pull a woman into a relationship. They have their own look at the world, quite different from yours or mine."

"So what – am I supposed to find a boyfriend?"

"No, just don't give an impression that you want to be with those women forever."

"But I do want the forever."

"No, you don't. You just think you do. Look the truth in the eyes. You get amused by discoveries and conquests. Once you have your trophy, you don't care for her anymore."

Andrzej was quiet.

"Yeah, you only are happy with the beginning," Mark continued. "You are unable to make it into the middle not to mention last to the end. The fact that you love them all is not a lie at all but it isn't the truth either. Your love simply has not appeared yet in your life."

"What are you talking about?" Andrzej cut him off.

"You asked me for an opinion so listen to the end."

Andrzej got silent.

"Stop looking for love. It will come on its own."

"So what am I supposed to do?"

"I've got an idea."

"What? Tell me," Andrzej got excited now.

"I think I have found my love."

Andrzej looked at him with a smile.

"I know. I saw you two in the hallway. You're right, that is love or at least looks like it. I know Kasia and I have never seen her 'in heaven'. When you held her hand, it was obvious that she was yours and entirely yours, only for you. I have to tell you that it was a very pleasant view to see the two of you like this."

"What you're saying is very nice and I thank you," Mark said. "I've never felt more assured and happier. This came so suddenly that I had no time to think about anything."

"Don't think!" Andrzej yelled. "Don't think. This is what I do and this is exactly why I am lost. Don't think, just live."

"You're right. I decided to live. I am not going to plan anymore or analyze. I do have a lot to do and many duties that take a great deal of my time. I have decided then that I can sort of dump those obligations on you and this way I will have the time for Kasia."

"Wait a minute, what duties?" Andrzej got stunned.

"Well, for a while now I have felt like I am responsible for what's going on in the world. I don't like when ignorance and greed takes over the common sense."

"I agree," Andrzej nodded.

"I help therefore; I help people and institutions to straighten out some situations."

"Straighten out?"

"Yes. I will explain it to you later. I would like that you start to do what I have been doing."

"You'll have to," Andrzej stared. "I can't just accept an offer from a guy I have met an hour earlier and who, on top of that, has fallen in love."

Mark burst out laughing.

"Let's start with this," he said. He pulled out from his pocket a checkbook and showed it to Andrzej. Andrzej looked and after a moment jumped away as if struck by a thunder. He was looking at Mark not saying anything.

"Should I continue?" Mark asked.

"You don't have to. I accept," Andrzej answered seriously.

"I am glad you took upon my offer. As a token of appreciation I will leave you a souvenir." Mark took off of his hand the golden Rolex, took Andrzej's hand and put the watch on his wrist. Andrzej was quiet. He knew this was the beginning of his new road.

Music kept on going especially spicy. The flashes of lights kept cooling down the dancers' extravaganzas and the thoughts of the tempted. The club was full of life and full of music. Two strangers found each other in this great big world. Love came to be and justice and common sense will take off on a journey with greed and deceit. Who will win? There are no winners in this competition and there are no losers. There is no truth and no lie. It is only us, and us alone – the people; ordinary and not so ordinary.

Once we truly begin to love life as it is, the spark of hope will shine.

The End

www.ingramcontent.com/pod-product-compliance
Lightning Source LLC
Chambersburg PA
CBHW060522100426
42743CB00009B/1403